# AGILE
## for Instructional Designers

## Iterative
## Project Management
## to Achieve Results

## Megan Torrance

ATD Press is an internationally renowned source of insightful and practical information on
talent development, training, and professional development.

**ATD Press**
1640 King Street
Alexandria, VA 22314 USA

**Ordering information:** Books published by ATD Press can be purchased by visiting ATD's
website at www.td.org/books or by calling 800.628.2783 or 703.683.8100.

Library of Congress Control Number: 2019943505

ISBN-10: 1-949036-50-2
ISBN-13: 978-1-949036-50-3
e-ISBN: 978-1-94903-651-0

**ATD Press Editorial Staff**
Director: Sarah Halgas
Manager: Melissa Jones
Community of Practice Manager, Learning Development: Eliza Blanchard
Developmental Editor: Jack Harlow
Production Editor: Hannah Sternberg
Text and Cover Design: Shirley E.M. Raybuck
Cover Design: Darrin Raaum

Printed by Color House Graphics, Grand Rapids, MI

# Contents

# Introduction

The first time the term Agile was used to describe an iterative development process specific to software was with the Agile Manifesto written in February 2001. The Agile process aimed to make it easier for software engineers, their teams, and their business sponsors to work together and be adaptive, resulting in a better product for the end user.

But the concepts underlying Agile have much earlier roots. Some argue that Agile traces all the way back to the 1620s with the development of the scientific method by Francis Bacon. A more commonly thought of starting point is the Plan-Do-Study-Act (PDSA) cycle developed by Walter Shewhart in the 1930s. PDSA, like Agile, is an iterative and incremental development methodology that was adapted and used to train hundreds of managers at Toyota in the 1950s (Rigby, Sutherland, and Takeuchi 2016).

In the 1980s and 1990s, with the explosion of software development as an industry, leaders continued their search for better processes. Studies showed that teams who worked together and continued to refresh their design and development processes created more successful innovations much more quickly than their competitors. Two of the people at the forefront of this work were Jeff Sutherland and Ken Schwaber, who created the Scrum method, named after a rugby move in which players pack tightly together and move as one in an attempt to gain possession of the ball. Scrum had the same goals that Agile ultimately would: finishing projects on time, under budget, and with fewer bugs. Sutherland and Schwaber were then involved in the creation of the Manifesto for Agile Software Development (the Agile Manifesto) in 2001.

## The Agile Manifesto

The Agile Manifesto shapes the work of Agile project management teams. Unlike other manifestos, this one is quite short but no less powerful. A mere 68 words, the Agile Manifesto lays out these core values:

> We are uncovering better ways of developing software by doing it and helping others do it. Through this work we have come to value:
> - individuals and interactions over processes and tools
> - working software over comprehensive documentation
> - customer collaboration over contract negotiation
> - responding to change over following a plan.
>
> That is, while there is value in the items on the right, we value the items on the left more.

The Agile Manifesto reflects collaborative, practical values and a desire to approach project management in a way that focuses on people—both the people who make up the project team and the end users of the product. What it means for L&D in practice is:

- listening to team members and stakeholders and changing the product's look, feel, and features in response to feedback and changing needs; being willing to revisit and repeat phases, such as design and development, following iterative implementations and feedback
- prioritizing delivery of a responsive app that performs the tasks a learner needs over a complete, perfect, beautifully formatted project scope, technical manual, and set of interface specs—or a set of detailed wireframes or storyboards imagining the potential (but nonexistent) app

- revisiting lists of deliverables as the project evolves rather than holding to (and billing for) each item on the list whether it is ultimately needed or not
- adjusting the schedule if a member of the team is reassigned or unexpectedly absent

Thanks to these values, Agile has since become ubiquitous amid any team or organization developing software. Beyond the four core values, Agile teams follow a set of 12 principles, which turn a short and sweet statement of intention into actionable directions. These 12 Agile principles are:

1. Our highest priority is to satisfy the customer through early and continuous delivery of valuable software.
2. Welcome changing requirements, even late in development. Agile processes harness change for the customer's competitive advantage.
3. Deliver working software frequently, from a couple of weeks to a couple of months, with a preference to the shorter timescale.
4. Business people and developers must work together daily throughout the project.
5. Build projects around motivated individuals. Give them the environment and support they need, and trust them to get the job done.
6. Face-to-face conversation is the most efficient and effective method of conveying information to and within a development team.
7. Working software is the primary measure of progress.
8. Agile processes promote sustainable development. The sponsors, developers, and users should be able to maintain a constant pace indefinitely.
9. Continuous attention to technical excellence and good design enhances agility.

10. Simplicity—the art of maximizing the amount of work not done—is essential.

11. The best architectures, requirements, and designs emerge from self-organizing teams.

12. At regular intervals, the team reflects on how to become more effective, then tunes and adjusts its behavior accordingly.

These 12 principles can easily apply to the L&D world too. In the appendix, I've detailed how I adapted each one specifically for developing learning projects; check it out now, or reference it as needed throughout this book.

## My History With Agile

My own career paralleled the emergence of Agile in the software industry. In the 1990s, as a project manager at Andersen Consulting (now Accenture) and Arthur Andersen, I followed their Method/1: Plan-Design-Develop-Implement, with evaluation left for the next plan phase (Rifkin 1992). Glorious in its detail and rigid in its implementation, Method/1 and I had a rather stressful love/hate relationship. But brute force and long hours could overcome any project management deficiency when you're in your 20s and don't know any better!

After leaving the firm and starting my own consultancy around LMS implementation and e-learning development in the early 2000s, I abandoned the rigid project planning ethos because my work in instructional design was "so much more creative." And so I spent just as much brute force and long hours, just without a solid project plan.

As my company, TorranceLearning, grew and our client projects got bigger, our loose approach to project management became unsustainable. Our clients were still happy with the results, but our work-life balance was out of control. Midway through a project, we had no idea if we would finish on time, if we would have to write off hours we couldn't possibly bill the client, or if we'd be able to keep up with a constantly shifting set of needs and requirements along the way. We needed to do something better.

By happenstance, my social and business networking circle included a lot of software developers, and by this time Agile was becoming the norm in our local tech scene. I spent time with Dianne Marsh of SRT Solutions, Helene Gidley of HSG Consulting, Rich Sheridan of Menlo Innovations, Marisa Smith of the Whole Brain Group, and Rob Houck of LearnShare, soaking up what they were doing on their projects. This was 2008. Each of these small businesses had their own approach to Agile. Their similarities were helpful foundations, while their differences inspired us to make our own adaptations for the instructional design space.

In late 2011, we realized these adaptations were quite extensive. Our business model and way of engaging with our clients was fully wrapped around our project management approach. We wondered if the extent of our changes still qualified us as using Agile. We decided to call it the Lot Like Agile Management Approach and named it LLAMA®.

LLAMA works for us. It works for clients. And we felt like we had something to share with our peers. The TorranceLearning team and I have been sharing this approach with fellow L&D professionals since 2012. By now, thousands of people have learned about LLAMA and adopted it in whole or in part to their work.

In the middle of writing this book, Susan Lord, a courseware developer and project manager who attended a LLAMA workshop at a conference wrote this to me:

> Hi! I just wanted to tell you I did my first Agile chart with Post-its and tape on my wall. . . . It is enormous but I am no longer drowning. I got my team on board and they can visualize what is needed. Thank you, thank you!

It outlines our process flows, what milestone we are at, and what needs to happen to complete this phase. And what is wonderful is there was no bossing anyone around. Which I love! Everyone was in it! Fantastic!

I also found out my manager was in your class last month. So we are now speaking the same language.

This quick exchange over LinkedIn sums up many of the appealing aspects of Agile and LLAMA: the clarity of visible project management, team engagement, work-directed teams, and a shared vision with teams, leaders, and their business sponsors. These aspects are within your reach too.

## Who This Book Is For

I've written this book for all the instructional designers, course developers, learning experience designers, and other professionals leading projects in the learning and development or training space who are looking to find a better way to manage their projects and deliver better results, on time and in budget. Essentially, a better way to work. Our industry is not steeped in a project management culture, yet nearly all the work we do is done as a project, with a defined start and end date and a deliverable to be produced. The model we've followed for a half century or so—the ADDIE model—no longer serves us in a do-more-with-less world of constant change.

Whether you're creating instructor-led facilitated experiences, virtual classroom training, e-learning, performance support, mobile learning apps, or advanced digital learning experiences, your work is somewhat like the work of software developers. And the approach outlined in this book borrows heavily from the Agile approach used the software industry.

# What's in This Book

The book opens with chapter 1, which lays out the case for using Agile in an L&D context. It highlights where the traditional waterfall approach to project management (ADDIE) fails to respond to changing demands. It also presents my Lot Like Agile Management Approach, which adjusts Agile in ways to make it a better fit for instructional design.

Then, part 1 describes the project kickoff and setting a project up for success with Agile. Chapter 2 guides you through planning the project kickoff, including who needs to participate and what do you need to cover during it. Chapter 3 covers how you should define the project's goal, particularly whether it should be training or performance focused. Chapter 4 delves into how to craft personas from your learner base, then how to select the primary learner on which your training will focus. Chapter 5 borrows the concept of user stories from software development to help you define scope. Chapter 6 takes a different approach to scope definition, one more suitable to instructional projects, and offers the Action Mapping technique, which you can use to identify key behaviors related to the goal, then map activities and content to those behaviors.

Part 2 moves into the routine of actually managing the project. Here, you'll learn how to define tasks and deliver iterations of the product, as well as establish a sustainable working rhythm with your Agile team. Chapter 7 shows you how to plan for an iterative project, including lining up the high-level arc of the project with your daily workflow while anticipating the unexpected. Chapter 8 details the challenges in estimating tasks, and then  presents four rules for dealing with said challenges. Chapter 9 gets into the core component of an Agile project, the iteration; it makes the case for why iterative design works and presents ways to get it right. Chapter 10 digs into the rhythms that govern Agile projects as well as how to work well with subject matter experts and Agile software teams. Because open, regular communication is essential to Agile success, chapter 11 focuses on how you can ensure you're communicating in the right fashion with the right people. Chapter 12 examines the transformative power of the retrospective, both during iterations in the middle of the project and as debriefs once it's wrapped up.

Throughout the first two parts, the book discusses Agile as implemented on a single project. Finally, part 3 places Agile in a broader organizational context where multiple projects compete for attention. Chapter 13 shows you how to scale Agile beyond one project to manage and prioritize multiple Agile projects at once. Chapter 14 wraps up the book with a call to action for shifting the culture in your team, department, or organization to lay the groundwork for Agile. The appendixes contain ready-to-use job aids for applying the techniques in the book to your projects as well as a more detailed look at how each of the 12 principles of Agile can be applied to L&D. I recommend flipping back to it from time to time as you read and each principle comes into play.

Welcome to the world of Agile and LLAMA. I hope this book offers you the techniques and mindset for embracing a new way of working. Just as our projects are iterative and incremental when we use Agile, this method is as well. I welcome your engagement and feedback any time!

# CHAPTER 1

# The Case for Agile

## In This Chapter
- Where does ADDIE fall short?
- What is Agile project management?
- How can Agile work for instructional design?

A woman approached the TorranceLearning booth at a conference several years ago.

She said, "Megan! I hear that you help people with their project management problems. I need your help."

I adjusted my cape, stood a little bit taller, and asked her about the problem.

She said, "You have to help me stop the 11th-hour changes!"

That made me pause a little bit. I wasn't sure how to respond.

She clearly didn't know that my whole project management "thing" was about accepting and expecting changes, even late in the project.

I asked her what she was making training about.

"Software."

I asked what kept changing.

"The software."

Was she really trying to stop the development of a product so that she could be on time and within budget with her part of the project? Even at the risk of delivering some-

thing that was wrong? Probably not. And yet the framing of her question—stopping change so she can finish her work—is probably familiar to many of us in L&D.

This anecdote illustrates the biggest problems with how instructional designers have managed projects for years. The focus has been on the wrong things: It's all about delivering something—anything—on schedule and within budget. Not that those are bad goals, but they leave a critical factor out of the equation: the learners. Your on-time, on-budget piece of training might not work. It might not do what the learners need. It might not meet the learning objectives.

Let's put learners back in focus for our instructional design projects. But first, we need to clarify precisely why traditional project management methods are inadequate.

## What's Wrong With ADDIE?

The stalwart of learning and development project management is ADDIE, a decades-old linear or "waterfall" approach to planning and managing software and instructional design projects (Figure 1-1). ADDIE describes the five phases of project planning: analysis, design, development, implementation, and evaluation. While there's nothing inherently wrong with that formula, when applied literally ADDIE assumes a linear progression from one phase to the next. Once one phase is complete, the project team moves to the next phase. Generally, there is no opportunity to revisit earlier phases; a developer can't climb back up the waterfall.

**Figure 1-1.** The ADDIE Workflow

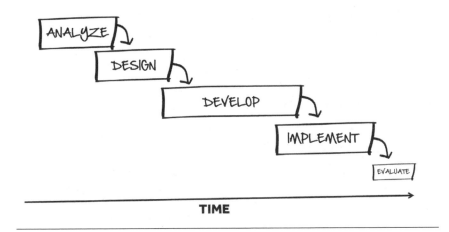

In a model like this, if you go back to the drawing board it's because something went horribly wrong. Even more problematic, in a waterfall model, evaluation occurs only at the end. This leaves the end users' experience out of the design and development process. It also means that if problems or flaws in the design or implementation are found, they cannot easily be remedied. Problems wait to be fixed until the next product update, which could be months (or years) away, or they entail extremely costly changes, late delivery, and huge cost overruns.

One of my mentors used to say that the first day of a project is the worst day to plan what the end product will be, how much it will cost, and how long it will take to get there. ADDIE works fine . . . if nothing in your project changes from the day you draft the project plan to the day you deliver the training. But how often does that happen? Right: almost never.

For example, what if the technology changes during development? What if the target audience of trainees is assigned new or different goals, and the learning objectives for the training change dramatically? As any instructional designer or developer knows, change is:

- scary
- frustrating
- inevitable
- happening faster than ever.

It's also:

- exciting
- an opportunity
- another word for improvement.

It's quite likely your project needs to change over time because the project requestor's or sponsor's needs evolve in tandem with the underlying business needs, as clients learn more about the learning experience or as ideas are tried and tested. To assume otherwise is to set yourself up for failure. It's folly to assume that the project sponsors know everything they want at the beginning of a project.

Rather than avoiding and fearing change or, like the desperate woman at the conference, attempting to prevent it, why not embrace change? Accept that it is inevitable, expect it in all your projects, and welcome changes as opportunities to make better products.

The truth of it is that everyone—the development team and the sponsors—is learning more about the project as it unfolds. And, quite frankly, it's often the instructional designers on the team who are coming up with new ideas as the project grows. (If you're not, you may not be fully engaged in the work you're doing!)

## ADDIE: A Relic of a Never-Existent Era

ADDIE hails from a bygone—and completely mythical—era when (if you just planned your project carefully and thoroughly enough) design, development, and implementation would progress smoothly, reaching a scheduled, on-budget, happily-ever-after ending. Learners would get what they needed from the training, and the project team would cheerfully move on to the next neat, plannable project.

L&D professionals understand that to be just what it is: a fairy tale. While models like ADDIE can work in product manufacturing or construction, the linear waterfall model is inappropriate for product or learning development—or any innovative process. Processes with high variability simply cannot be pinned down in a plan written before design has begun.

Real-life project planning for training is a little bumpier than planning to manufacture countless identical products using a predictable process. Planning, designing, and developing L&D programs calls for the flexibility not only to adapt to change but to anticipate and welcome change, whether it's changing demands of project sponsors, changing preferences of learners, or changing business needs of organizations.

Only by testing incremental releases or partially complete products can you catch errors, clumsy features, and potentially disastrous problems early in the development cycle. By failing early, you can fix them relatively easily compared with the consequences of discovering a fatal flaw only when the final product is in the hands of hundreds or thousands of learners.

The solution? An iterative model like Agile project management.

## What Is Agile?

Agile is a team-based project management approach that emphasizes iteration and openness to change. An Agile team experiments and observes—and tests and gathers feedback on—a product as it is developed. Agile is ideal for projects where business needs might change, where specifications are not well defined at the outset, and where decisions are complex and require creativity. Agile builds in flexibility by:

- building deliverables in small increments
- releasing usable (testable) products multiple times during the development process
- applying feedback on the early releases to improve successive iterations.

Before getting into how Agile translates to instructional design, let's start with my own concise definition: Agile is an iterative, incremental method of guiding design and building projects in a highly flexible and interactive manner, focusing on maximizing customer value and fostering high team engagement.

## The Lot Like Agile Management Approach

My definition of Agile fits in perfectly with my Agile approach adapted specifically for instructional design: LLAMA, or Lot Like Agile Management Approach. It is iterative and incremental (training to be tested, evaluated, and revised during design and development, rather than at the end). It guides design and build projects (remember Agile isn't an instructional design method itself and should not supplant best practices in that area). It is highly flexible (you need to be willing and able to respond to changes throughout the process). It is interactive (the team, the sponsor, and the subject matter experts work together). It maximizes customer value (your job is not to simply create training and move on to the next thing—you have to ensure your process delivers value to the customer, the end user). And it fosters high team engagement (whether you are a department of one or part of a multi-person function, you will need to engage a team of sponsors, stakeholders, subject matter experts, and learners to succeed).

This doesn't mean we need to throw away ADDIE entirely. The LLAMA approach includes the phases of ADDIE, with a twist (Figure 1-2).

**Figure 1-2.** ADDIE Adapted for Agile

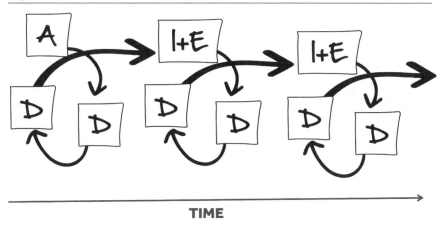

**TIME**

Rather than assuming that the initial analysis covered everything and that no changes will be requested during design and development, Agile continuously returns to the design and development phases after successive evaluations. Rather than creating a single final product, Agile teams create multiple iterations. Projects are completed in small increments. In each phase, a product is created that stakeholders and learners can see, test, play with, and even break. This gives teams the chance to identify problems they hadn't anticipated or reevaluate features or functions that might not work in practice as they had envisioned.

It's also a way to accommodate changes that occur for reasons other than design errors. Maybe the end users' managers decided to buy tablets for all their sales personnel, and now the performance support tool has to work on mobile. Maybe a new product or a major upgrade demands additional training. Newly discovered information could render training methods or content obsolete.

The point is, the development team and the project management team cannot prevent change. And it's not possible to know everything about a project in the initial design phase; nor is it reasonable to expect to anticipate all possible changes. What those teams can do is build in a way to respond to the inevitable changes.

Agile project management offers that flexibility and keeps the focus on the end user by emphasizing evaluation throughout. This phase, at the very end of ADDIE, often gets neglected. Here's how the evaluation discussion typically plays out, whether you're developing software or training: A project is done; it's been a long slog, but the team has delivered, finally! The last thing anyone wants to hear is what's wrong with the product. Any changes needed won't be implemented until the product is updated anyhow. So why spend time or money evaluating it?

With Agile for software development, evaluation is an essential part of each iteration. The feedback from the evaluation (the user testing or stakeholder review) is applied to the next round of design, development, and implementation. These cycles repeat until the product is done to everyone's satisfaction, until a hard deadline is reached, or until the budget is exhausted.

But, you might be thinking, project planning for an instructional design project is not exactly like project planning for a software product. That's true! It's important to highlight some of the differences:

First, planning an instructional design project requires a focus on learning objectives and desired performance outcomes, not just on software features and functions. An Agile team breaks up a development project into "user stories"—small, manageable units of work. L&D teams similarly break big projects into smaller units, but these are based on learning objectives. A unit of work might be a single learner activity or a content object. Each story or "task" card includes information on who is doing the task and how long it will take.

Second, unlike software development teams, which tend to be dedicated to a single project at a time, many L&D teams are working simultaneously on multiple training and performance support products. This poses difficulties in planning that a dedicated software team is unlikely to encounter; however, the built-in flexibility of the Agile approach comes to the rescue here.

The Agile method involves breaking down large projects into very small pieces called stories. Team members estimate the amount of time each story will take. Thus a project schedule begins to emerge from these groups of stories.

LLAMA, like Agile, builds in tolerance for error. The time estimates are, after all, estimates. Schedules change; staff changes, gets sick, or goes on vacation. A task might take longer than expected. A needed content expert might be called away to deal with problems on another project. There's no way to plan for every contingency. But as long as clear, constant communication—an essential element of Agile and LLAMA—is the norm, this approach allows teams to get a realistic picture of who is needed when and for how long.

Third, L&D teams tend to consist of specialists; those who craft the learning objectives or provide the actual training content are often not developers. Even for digital learning projects, team members with software engineering and coding expertise might not have any instructional design knowledge. This specialization might lead to another key difference: The developers might have to wait for input from instructional designers or content experts at various stages in the development process.

That's where LLAMA comes in. Rather than trying to force an incompatible process to fit the Agile formula, LLAMA adjusts Agile in ways that make it a better fit for instructional design project management. In this book, I will extend the case I've just made for Agile for instructional designers by showing you how you can kick off the project the right way (part 1), then manage it through multiple iterations (part 2). By the end, I hope you will become your own advocate for why Agile makes sense in your organization!

# An Interview With Emily Ricco, Learning & Development Manager, HubSpot

**When and why did you decide to use Agile?**

I've been with HubSpot's Learning & Development team since 2014. When I recognized the opportunity for greater focus on learning design and content creation, I started an instructional design group. A few months after that, I adopted Agile because we had a long list of projects to tackle and very few people dedicated to tackling them. I wanted to empower this new team to take ownership of their work and how they got that work done. At the same time, I wanted to ensure we had strong communication and collaboration and could keep up with the pace of the business areas we supported. After doing some research, I discovered Scrum and related to the principles behind it: transparency, inspection, and adaptation. Two out of three of those principles are part of HubSpot's culture code, so it seemed a natural fit.

**What barriers did you have to overcome?**

I had to find the right version of Agile that would work for our team and our business. Everyone has their own opinions about Agile. Everything I read in articles and books and everyone I spoke with at other companies only increased the number of opinions to consider. Additionally, it was an entirely new way to work, and I had to strike the balance of avoiding micromanagement while ensuring consistent communication and structure.

**How does your organization's culture support Agile (or not)?**

Our organization's culture supports Agile because it is fast-paced and transparent. Agile allows us to set expectations and move quickly, which in turn allows us to be better partners. Transparency and adaptability are part of HubSpot's Culture Code, as well as part of the principles behind Scrum.

**Do you have a story to share about describing Agile to someone else?**

Our L&D team is mainly centralized but historically other teams have wanted to take charge of their own learning and development in order to move at a quicker pace. Last year, I used Agile as a way to build trust with one of those teams. I wanted to convince them that we were the right partners to work with on their ongoing training. When I described the opportunity they would have for providing feedback and the level of communication and transparency, the stakeholders were excited and confident in our ability to deliver. They even ended up providing headcount on our team from their budget so we could continue to partner with them and support them in a greater way.

# Key Takeaways

- A linear, waterfall-shaped approach to project management fails to incorporate the inevitable changes a project will face and sets up the project team for a struggle to manage those changes.
- An iterative, incremental approach like Agile accommodates change and offers a framework for meeting project needs while maintaining appropriate control of timeline and budget considerations.
- The Lot Like Agile Management Approach, or LLAMA, is an Agile approach adapted specifically for instructional design projects.

# Part 1:
## Kicking Off the Project

# Plan the Kickoff

In This Chapter
- Why kick off an Agile project?
- Who do you invite to the kickoff session?
- What does a kickoff agenda look like?

"Megan, I know this isn't the kind of project you want, but we could really use some quick help," a client, Jim, said over phone.

"Sure, how can we help?" I replied, because that's what I'm in the business of doing.

"I have three PowerPoint decks for the same workshop, each created by a different instructor. Can you just combine the three into one that looks good, and make us a facilitator guide

so they can be consistent going forward? There aren't any changes to the course itself. Seriously, I'm just asking you to put lipstick on my pig. We're rebuilding the entire workshop later, but this needs to be our stopgap."

Since this seemed like a relatively straightforward, practically administrative task, we didn't insist on our regular project kickoff session. I asked Jim to send over the three sets of files and we got to work.

After several iterations and two months of work, we weren't getting anywhere. Nothing we produced in this seemingly simple project was what the client wanted, but we couldn't figure out what the right answers were. We were burning through our timeline—and the client's patience.

"Jim, this just isn't working. Let's start all over. Can we schedule a project kickoff meeting?"

"Two months into the project?"

"Exactly."

And that's what we did. We started back at the beginning, defining the organization's goal, the learners' goals, who the learners actually were, and the scope of the project. The four hours we spent kicking off the project—even two months late—were incredibly valuable. We found out that what Jim really wanted was a different course, not lipstick on his pig. It was the project kickoff session that helped him discover that.

Now, every project gets a kickoff.

## Kicking Off an Agile Project

We're going to spend the next five chapters discussing the kickoff for an Agile project. While this step is miniscule in terms of the overall time spent on the project, it will likely result in the most valuable several hours you spend. In the project kickoff session, you will work out the project's goals, measures, scope, risks, resource needs, cost estimates, high-level schedule, and approaches to getting there, ideally with all the relevant parties in the room and in agreement. Before you can actually meet a vision for success, it's critical for everyone to define and agree upon that vision together.

The agenda and time spent on each item in the kickoff can vary according to the project's size and need. The larger and more complex a project is, the more important it is to thoroughly prepare and start with shared goals and expectations. I have seen project kickoff sessions last from two hours (for a half hour of instruction) to two days (for a multi-week curriculum).

Stepping back even further for a moment, it's common for project teams to prepare a great deal before the project kickoff session. Most organizations spend weeks or months of planning, defining requirements, conducting analysis, allocating resources, budgeting, and perhaps selecting vendors before the kickoff. The specifics of this preparation work also depend on the organization and the project. In other cases, teams do very little in advance short of identifying a working title for the product to be developed.

## Introducing Your Team to Agile

As important as it is to ensure that those on an extended project team (sponsor, stakeholders, SMEs, and so on) are on board with an Agile approach, it's absolutely critical that your team be on the same page with respect to terminology, processes, principles, and tools when implementing LLAMA. Depending on your team size and approach, there are a few ways to get started:

If you're a team of one, you can just get started. Read this book. Check out some of the many resources available on the Internet or local Agile or professional groups, and get started with a project that lends itself well to Agile.

If you're on a larger team, getting organized and level-set may involve attending a workshop together or working with a consultant, or simply identifying one person as the Agile or LLAMA lead in your organization and having that person head the change effort. Most of the time when I am called in to lead a workshop, it's because a team has recently reorganized or had some other catalyst for change. The workshop is the introduction for the whole team, and then they decide how best to implement Agile in their organization.

A go-slow-to-go-fast strategy would be to take an Agile approach to implementing Agile. Choose a project and form a pilot team to get started, figure out some things about how Agile adapts to your workflow, then get the whole team involved at a second or third project iteration.

# Who Is Invited to the Kickoff?

The kickoff session—and the project itself—is most effective when the right people are engaged in the process from the start. People are busy and schedules are tight, but the organization's ability to make a commitment to getting all the players together for a project kickoff signals the high priority placed on the project. There will be other times when you have to make do without everyone in the room, and that's OK. How many people should be there? That varies greatly depending on the nature, complexity, and size of the project, and the norms of the organization. Ideally, these people are involved in the project kickoff:

## The Project Sponsor

The project sponsor sets the goal for the project, has the authority to allocate resources, decides priorities for scope and resources, and often gives the final approval for project release and completion. The sponsor may or may not be a subject matter expert in the content to be trained. This person (known by software teams that use Agile as the product owner) is typically a business owner of the project, and often the senior-most leader involved in the project. If it's unclear who the sponsor is, it's often the person whom the participants in the learning experience you are creating report to, either directly or through the organization hierarchy.

In some cases, the project sponsor is not the final decision maker or is not from the business. For example, the final decision maker might not be able to commit the time required of project sponsor, so someone else is selected to play that role. That person has most of the authority when it comes to day-to-day or week-to-week decisions about the project but may need to check in with the senior leader for bigger decisions.

Less often, the project sponsor is a senior member of the L&D team. This works when that person is very close to the business needs and has direct access to decision makers.

The project sponsor, whomever it ends up being, is a required attendee at the kickoff session. If this person is unavailable, you may need to schedule around the sponsor's calendar to ensure he or she can attend.

## Project Stakeholders

Stakeholders are anyone or any group that will affect (or be affected by) the project or the resulting training to be delivered. The distinction between the sponsor and the stakeholders is that while stakeholders have influence on the decision, the sponsor is the one who makes the final decision.

For an instructional design project, stakeholders may include:

- other representatives from the organization
- other organization units that may also use this training
- human resources
- recruiting
- instructors
- LMS administrators
- IT and helpdesk support
- internal communications
- marketing.

Project stakeholders are not required attendees at the kickoff session, although they are certainly invited. As the facilitator of the kickoff session, your role is to ensure that the stakeholders' considerations are taken into account while still leaving decision-making authority to the business sponsor, even in a consensus-based organization. If one or more project stakeholders is not present at the kickoff session, you will need to identify how best to communicate to them the results of the session and the project's plan going forward.

## Subject Matter Experts

Subject matter experts (SMEs) are a special class of project stakeholders in that they are the keepers of the knowledge that is the content of the training you are about to build. SMEs are critical resources for the project once it gets started and may even be members of the project team. Keep in mind that some SMEs, because of their expert status, may not actually perform the tasks that your training project is addressing.

Most SMEs will have no formal instructional design experience or Agile project management experience. Since they are key players in your project going forward, you may want to take extra care to ensure that they are on board with your approach and the difference between their role as an expert in the content and your role as an expert in instructional design, as well as your role as a project manager using Agile.

At least one SME is a required participant in the project kickoff session. When a project has multiple SMEs, be sure to identify their respective or overlapping areas of expertise.

## Project Managers

It's quite likely that this your role and why you're reading this book. The project manager is the team lead with the responsibility for getting the work done. When working with an outside vendor, most organizations have an internal project manager who directs the work of the vendor, and the vendor has its own project manager assigned to lead the work of the design and delivery team.

For obvious reasons, the project manager is required at the kickoff session (both of them, when a vendor partner is used). Usually this person facilitates the session.

## Project Team Members

Most project managers will want to involve key members of the project team in the kickoff session. This helps to build solid relationships with the organizational leadership present and engage the team in the shared vision for the project going forward. Depending on the nature of the project, these team members may include people with the following roles or titles:

- instructional designer
- learning experience designer
- e-learning course developer
- software developer
- learning engineer
- graphic designer
- editor/quality assurance
- facilitator/trainer
- training operations specialist
- LMS administrator.

## Learners

The people who are in the target learner population for the project have an important voice in the training project, but they are often overlooked as participants in the kickoff session. In instances where the SMEs and business sponsor are removed from the day-to-day work skills your project is addressing, this connection to the learner becomes even more important. Depending on the project, representatives of the learner population could include someone who is:

- performing the work now
- currently in training
- doing the task in a different setting
- learning in a different modality than the one your project will address
- recently learned this topic and is now applying it on the job.

It may simply not be feasible to include representatives of the learners themselves in the kickoff session. In that case, you may grab someone from this list of proxy learners:

- Instructors, trainers, or facilitators who teach this topic to the target audience currently have a good grasp of the content, the learners, and the sticking points in training today. Note, however, that some instructors may not actually perform the work or they may be SMEs, either of which makes them qualitatively different from the learners themselves.
- Immediate supervisors of the people who will be performing this work have often been in the learners' role in the past. Their expertise stems from their role in evaluating good and bad performance on the job and in the business.
- Help desk or customer service personnel who support the learners in this particular topic or task have keen and detailed insight into the struggles that learners face when implementing new skills on the job. Like instructors and supervisors, however, they may not perform the job itself. Further, help desk and customer service teams often only hear about things when they don't work—and they make lack insight to all the successes that occur and therefore don't require a service inquiry.

## Does the Project Kickoff Session Have to Be Done Face-to-Face?

Ideally the project kickoff session is done face-to-face, as that is the greatest bandwidth and highest resolution channel for people to communicate. However, with good planning and solid technology tools, the kickoff session can be done virtually. Here are some best practices for virtual kickoff sessions, which you may find strikingly similar to effective virtual classroom instruction:

- Make heavy use of visuals. Share the official note-taking screen with the group so everyone is aware of the details being recorded. And, since notes are taken live during the session, post-meeting follow-up is made all that much easier.
- Separate the role of facilitator and producer. Just like delivering in a virtual classroom, having a producer who can make sure that the right screens are

displayed at the right times and helping with participants' technical issues frees up the facilitator to guide the meeting. Often the producer is also a notetaker.

- Have two notetakers. One notetaker screenshares for all to see and makes the official set of notes for the meeting. The second notetaker is responsible for noting things that may be helpful for the instructional design process later on, but that might not make it into the official record.
- Be patient. Many things take longer when in the virtual meeting space. Check to make sure that all the relevant voices are heard. Take breaks as needed.
- Record the meeting. (Ask for permission first.) This is one of the ways in which a virtual kickoff session can be better than a face-to-face one; you have an easy way to make a recording that you can refer to later on.

## The Kickoff Session Agenda

What follows is a set of typical items covered in a project kickoff session—for example, defining the learner, defining the scope, and defining instructional and project parameters—and a suggestion of how much time to spend on each. You can make additions or changes to suit each new project at hand. In most cases, the entire team—business sponsor and L&D leaders included—learns more about their business and needs as a result of this kickoff session, even if the project itself is not pursued. The Project Kickoff Session Agenda job aid in appendix B offers a sample kickoff session agenda, which we'll cover in greater depth in the next subsections.

### Introductions and Approach (15 Minutes)

Provide the outline for the session, any necessary logistics (Wi-Fi password, facilities, breaks, and so on), and an overview of roles for the meeting itself. (Toward the end of the session, after you've defined scope and high-level timelines, you can review roles for the project going forward.)

## Define the Business Problem and Business Goals (1 Hour)

This is where you and the kickoff group come to agreement about the desired outcomes for the project. In most projects, by time you get to the kickoff session, everyone feels plenty sure that they understand the business goal—otherwise why kick off a training project? However, you should still insist on doing it. In every new project you might uncover some nuance about the project goals that make you all feel like it has been an hour well spent.

If the project sponsor cannot attend the full kickoff session, this portion of the meeting is an essential one for the sponsor to be involved in. This can be a challenging part of the session for the project sponsor, stakeholders, and facilitator, so it's a good idea to take a break when you're done here. This gives the project team a chance to regroup and reflect briefly.

More details about this aspect of the project kickoff are to be found in chapter 3, Define the Goal.

## Define the Learner (1 Hour or More)

Next, you will create two to five learner personas and determine which is the primary and which may be a close runner-up. The primary learner persona will be the focus of the scoping activities to come and will be useful again when defining reviewers for each iteration of the project.

More details about this aspect of the project kickoff are to be found in chapter 4, Define the Learner.

## Define the Scope (1 Hour or More)

With the business problem, business goal, and learners defined, it's time to address the scope of the project. To determine scope, you'll need to answer these questions and others:

- What performance objectives will this project meet?

- What are the expected measurable outcomes?
- What content will be needed (in terms of breadth and depth)?
- How richly will each piece of content be addressed?
- About how long should this learning experience be?
- Which learner audiences are included?

It is just as important to define what is within scope as it is to define what is out of scope. You can employ several methods to do so. For larger projects, it takes more time; for small projects this goes pretty quickly.

For projects where you are defining requirements for learning platforms, apps, and physical spaces, scope is defined by writing user stories. These projects create "doing" deliverables and are best scoped out using this traditional software-inspired method. You can find out more about writing user stories in chapter 5, Define Scope With User Stories.

For projects where you are creating instructional or learning experiences—"teaching" deliverables—you can define scope using a technique derived from Cathy Moore's popular Action Mapping process, instead of the user stories. You can find out more about using this method of defining scope in chapter 6, Define Scope Using Action Mapping.

If you haven't already taken one, this is another good time for a break.

## Define Key Instructional Parameters (1 Hour)

At this point in the session, the group has done a lot of the heavy lifting that will be required during your time together. While everyone is thinking about the learners and the scope of the project, some quick topics can be covered, making for a nice cognitive break:

- **Change management.** Is this part of a larger change
  management effort? Will one be required to roll this training
  out? While the details may best be left to another session, this
  context is important to identifying the risks, resources, and
  timelines for this project.

- **Cross-cutting concepts.** What other messages need to be conveyed as undercurrents or subtle suggestions throughout the training? While these are often nice-to-have aspects of the final deliverable, their contribution to broader organizational goals is worth noting.
- **Overall branding and tone.** What branding, messaging, and tone should the training take? Is there an internal or external brand guide?
- **Pre- and post-course support.** How will you support the learner before and after training?
- **Assessment and evaluation.** How will learners be assessed? How will the program itself be evaluated?

## Define Key Project Parameters (1 Hour)

Next, you'll cover a few items that come up in nearly every project kickoff session and are not unique to learning projects, such as:

- **Risks and mitigation strategies.** What known factors present a risk for this project? What unknowns do we fear? How will we mitigate them? How will we address them when they come up?
- **Technical specifications.** Where will this be hosted? How will people find the training? Will this need to use SCORM, AICC, xAPI, or something else? What platform will be used? Are there any development tools that must (or must not) be used? Addressing these questions is particularly relevant to digitally delivered training.
- **Accessibility factors.** What approach should be taken to ensuring that the training is accessible to everyone who will need it?

## Defining Risks

Risk definition and management is a fairly common project management activity and much has been written about it. I particularly like Lou Russell's "quick and dirty risk assessment" in her book *Project Management for Trainers*, 2nd edition, as it is sufficient to handle the needs of most learning and development projects. In Lou's approach, the entire extended team at the kickoff individually answers these three questions on a scale of 1-10, then the answers are shared and discussed:

1. How big is this project compared with others you have been a part of?
   (1 = it's the smallest; 10 = it's the largest)
2. How stable are the requirements for this project compared with other projects you have been a part of?
   (1 = the needs are completely clear; 10 = the needs are undefined)
3. How large will the learning curve be for this project? For example, does new software, hardware, or processes have to be learned?
   (1 = no learning curve; 10 = a considerable learning curve)

I like to add a few additional questions to the consideration:

4. How much change do we expect will be needed over the course of the project?
5. How many other pieces of this project are already underway (and perhaps out of our control)?
6. What has our history been with this project sponsor or part of the organization?

Specific risks are then documented, managed, mitigated, or simply observed throughout the project.

Keep in mind that the project's overall risk is likely to change as the needs change, as the team solves problems, and as new changes come to light. Teams that keep a healthy eye on the specific risks as well as the overall risk profile of the project are more likely to be successful than those who create a list at the beginning but don't come back and manage them regularly.

# Overall Project Budget and Timeline (30 Minutes)

While the project budget is something that you might not review in the kickoff session (it is often created after this session now that you know the scope and parameters for the project), the overall timeline for the effort certainly is.

All projects are constrained by three factors, and in each project one of the three is the primary constraint:

- time (deadline, due date, and so on)
- budget (for either cash or resources)
- scope (which can be defined as breadth of content or the depth to which it is addressed or presented).

If you're thinking all three of these are equally critical, you're not alone. I would encourage you to explore the constraints a bit more with your project sponsor. You may use questions such as:

- "If we're at the end of the project and something comes up that absolutely needs to be included, can we extend the timeline? Or do we save that scope for later?"
- "How likely is it that the timeline for this will shift?"
- "If one of our risk factors affects the project negatively, can we go over budget to mitigate it or should we plan to change the scope?"

In some project kickoff sessions, you might simply ask which priority is the most important if it isn't already obvious. The project sponsor will let you know which is the most constraining factor. Or, to survey the broader kickoff session group, you can put *time, budget,* and *scope* on a whiteboard or flipchart and ask participants to vote using a hashmark or a sticker, then take a break. Some people might vote early while some might wait until no one is in the room to put up their mark. And some might wait to see how others voted before they weigh in. Whatever the results, it's an opportunity to open up a conversation about project constraints that will help you determine an overall timeline and project plan. (Note that the business team—sponsor, stakeholders, SMEs— participate in this decision, not the instructional design and development team.)

Finally, you should ask about any overall business cycles and timelines that will affect the project, such as:

- busy and slow periods for the organization
- busy and slow periods for key SMEs and reviewers
- other ongoing projects that use the same people and resources, particularly ones with higher priority than yours
- vacations and planned leaves.

The high-level timeline for the project will be covered more in chapter 7, Plan the Project.

## Iterations and Review Responsibilities (15-30 Minutes)

A key aspect of Agile and LLAMA is, of course, the iterative development. Following along with the high-level timeline for the project are the timing and roles for reviewing each of the iterations you will produce. Chapter 9 covers iterations in more detail.

Here in the project kickoff session, you'll establish reviewer groups and roles and rough timelines for when the reviews will take place and how long each review will take. Take into account reviews from each of these groups, as appropriate:

- SMEs
- stakeholders
- sponsor
- learners
- legal, quality assurance, HR, and other organizational units.

# What Could Possibly Go Wrong?

Common issues with project kickoffs include:

**The project sponsor is in the L&D team.** When the project sponsor is from the organization—rather than from the L&D team—he or she directly defines what the organization needs in terms of performance.

When the project sponsor doesn't have that direct business connection, the L&D team risks creating training that is misaligned with organizational needs, is poorly defined in scope, and requires excessive reviews and iterations to get right. L&D teams that get this right seek out an organization sponsor or project champion to get that business insight.

**The project sponsor won't participate in the kickoff.** The project sponsor plays a key role in defining scope and priorities for the project. When they cannot participate in the kickoff, the project may suffer from the lack of those insights. The sponsor's inability to schedule time for the kickoff may signal this project's relative priority to the organization, which is very important information. It's worth doing whatever you can to work with the project sponsor's schedule or seek a proxy.

**Suitable learner representatives don't attend the kickoff.** While sponsors and subject matter experts know the organization's goals and the content, the learner representatives have a deep connection with the people who don't know—and are the audience for this training. If they can't participate in the kickoff session, find ways to get their input early in the project.

**Scheduling over multiple dates.** Sometimes to accommodate the schedules of a variety of people, a project kickoff has to be scheduled in smaller chunks over multiple dates. This risks not only losing continuity, but also losing participants from session to session. Decisions made in earlier sessions may not be fully understood by participants of later sessions. If it has to be done this way, be sure to capture not only the decisions made but the spirit of the conversation that got you there for a healthy recap each time the kickoff session reconvenes.

## Key Takeaways

- The Agile project kickoff session sets up the project for success in creating a shared vision of scope in terms of the learner definition, what is to be accomplished, and the desired performance outcomes, as well as how the project will be run.

- Participants in a project kickoff session should include the project sponsor, key stakeholders, subject matter experts, project managers, project team members, and representatives of the learner population.

- The project kickoff typically takes two to six hours depending on the scope and size of the project, although it may be longer for very large projects.

# CHAPTER 3

# Define the Goal

A client once asked me for input as they were planning to update a course that was a considerable part of their new hire orientation. The company was very focused on quality, and all new hires attended this one-day class on quality. The course contained a wealth of information on the emergence of the quality movement, its roots in Japanese manufacturing practices, and the company's commitment to quality.

It was unclear what the new hire was supposed to do with this information, though, so I asked.

"Oh, that's on the last slide in the deck. If you see a quality problem, fix it if you can or notify your supervisor to find someone who can," the client replied.

A course as comprehensive as that took weeks (at least!) to develop. An instructor spent several days a month teaching that class. Hundreds of new hires spent an entire day taking the

class as part of all the other things that they learned when starting a new job with a new company. But in the end, the only performance-related take-away was stashed on the last slide, well after new hires likely had tuned out the course.

Later in the chapter, I'll show how a more clearly defined goal around performance may have avoided wasting the time of the instructional designer, instructors, and new hires.

## Define the Goal to Manage Scope

By time you get to the project kickoff meeting, most project sponsors will assume that the goal of the project has been determined. That's a logical-sounding conclusion because at this point someone has decided that learning and development needs to be involved, in some cases a lengthy build-versus-buy or RFP and vendor selection process has been completed, the team members have been defined, time has been carved out for the kickoff session, and everyone has shown up. Most people assume that the kickoff session should therefore be focused on content.

Instead, you should start the kickoff session by defining the goal of the project, generally spending an hour or more on this. It's not unusual for this to be a little surprising, maybe even off-putting for some (especially the subject matter experts waiting to hand over their binders and slide decks and manuals), but it's one of the most impactful hours that will be spent on the project. It should come as no surprise that without a solid and shared definition of the goal, the project team's ability to deliver the desired results are limited at best.

A solid definition of the goal isn't unique to Agile or LLAMA. There are many ways to do this, many levels at which a goal can be defined, and many resources available for project managers to learn about this, including the excellent book by Cathy Moore, *Map It!* (2017), in which she provides a framework for defining a goal that will help the team determine whether and when developing training is the right answer.

Rather than rehash all the ways you can define a goal (I'm trusting that you don't need yet another tutorial on SMART goals, and I'm also trusting that you will run out and buy Cathy Moore's book), I will share the unique aspects of goal setting as they apply to scope definition for LLAMA.

## The Goal Is (Almost) Never to Build Training

Some in the kickoff session will see the goal of the project as simply designing and developing some kind of training, with what happens after beyond the project's purview. That couldn't be more mistaken. Instead, the goal is usually to help people do their jobs better. Or to apply some concepts in their lives. Or to move forward to a more advanced topic. Building training is just the way that you meet that goal (maybe).

For example, consider two projects, one with a training design goal and another with a performance goal:

> **Training goal:** Train forklift drivers about safety.
> **Result:** The project team creates and rolls out a course to everyone about forklift safety.
>
> **Performance goal:** Forklift drivers will follow safety precautions and reduce accidents and near-misses.
> **Result:** The project team creates better warning signage, works with the warehouse to install mirrors and update the walkway

striping, and creates a course about forklift safety for new hires plus a quick "what's new" video for existing employees who know the old rules but not the updated ones.

By defining the goal around performance outcomes, you set the project team up for success. Instructional designers know that it's often not sufficient to simply design and deliver a course. A performance-based goal opens up that conversation and makes it more likely that your resulting training will be effective.

## Performance-Based Goals Help Contain Project Scope

Recall one of the Agile principles: Simplicity—the art of maximizing the amount of work not done—is essential.

The client in the beginning of this chapter was building a course about quality for new hires, but scope creep—the addition of new things to a project that potentially delay delivery and risk the quality of the course itself—became a real problem in a content-centric course. In this case (I'm assuming), a goal more focused on performance would have led to a shorter course to develop, deliver, and attend.

Therefore, a solid and shared definition of a performance-based goal becomes the first screening criterion for the inevitable new requests that come in during a project. When someone pokes their head over the cube wall and asks, "Can we mention XYZ in your course?" or sends you an email that suggests, "Let's include a whiteboard video explaining how we got to this point," your first question should be "How does this help meet the goal?"

## "Why Aren't They Doing It Now?"

Set yourself and your project up for success by closing out the goal-definition process with this simple question: Why aren't they doing it now?

Or, why aren't the participants doing what it is that you want them to do after the training?

Expect to hear a wide variety of interesting answers to this question:

- "The system requires 18 clicks to get there—and the path isn't clear."
- "They don't have the data to know they need to do it."
- "Their managers don't give them time to do it."
- "They are measured (or even compensated) for doing something contrary to this."

This question helps you out in a few ways. First, it identifies the aspects of performance that are not related to training, providing context for how much performance improvement can be expected from training. For example, a forklift safety training course won't improve safety much if there aren't clearly marked drive paths.

Second, the answers to this question provide insight into other initiatives that can be pursued to improve performance. Some of these ideas may involve additional deliverables for your team or may require getting other functions and departments involved. For example, you may have been brought on to create a one-time forklift safety e-learning course for new hires, but in your analysis of why operators aren't working safely right now, you discover that posting short job aids as signs throughout the facility and improving the positioning of corner mirrors would also contribute to the performance goal of improving safety. You may need to bring in other departments to address these things.

And third, you will learn how the goal is measured. Throughout the iterative development process you're about to embark on, you'll be measuring whether the deliverables you create have an impact on the performance. The kickoff meeting is an excellent time to gain an understanding about how the organization measures the performance, and in some cases, whether or not this performance is even being measured. If it turns out that this particular goal and its performance are not being measured, you should begin that measurement process. That will give you a benchmark against which to determine whether training deliverables that you create have provided any measurable benefit. It's hard to demonstrate you've improved forklift safety unless you have data on previous accidents.

# Defining an 80 Percent Goal

It is entirely likely that your discussion in the meeting will not result in a perfectly articulated goal. In fact, I find that that level of detail is not necessarily meaningful for the project team at the kickoff session. The purpose for the kickoff session is to arrive at a defined and shared goal, which the business can continue to refine after the session is done. This makes for efficient use of time because it is often the case that the final adjustments to the goal need to be made with people who may not be in the room for the kickoff.

But to not come away entirely empty handed, you need to ensure your goal hits a few key concepts. You will use your best judgement or defer to the project sponsor to make the call about whether a particular idea is worth diving into at very granular level or declaring it good enough and moving on. By defining a goal at about 80 percent readiness and telling the assembled kickoff team members that you are doing so, you relieve some of the inherent anxiety about perfectly defining something. You also communicate that the project team will be open to change and refinement over time and that you understand this is a normal process as the project unfolds.

## What's the Difference Between Scope Creep and Embracing Change?

Admittedly, there's a continuum between "scope creep" and "embracing change." Scope creep is generally considered a bad thing—the result of additional content and requirements added after the team and the sponsor have agreed to a scope of deliverables or constant requests for changes and refinements at the "end" of a project. Scope creep is frustrating to the project team because it's incredibly difficult to deliver on time and in budget if additional things are added without commensurate flexibility in delivery time and resources.

On the other hand, we've established that the underlying needs for most projects are evolving throughout the project and the team is learning from each iteration what works and what doesn't work, so the project scope should be changing. Embracing this kind of thing is good and often necessary, although it may also require a commensurate flexibility in delivery time and resources.

When faced with a request (internally or externally sourced) to change the project's scope in some way, we look at the source and nature of the request.

It might be scope creep (and "bad") if:
- You're adding content without any additional performance outcomes or related activities.
- You're making adjustments that do not materially affect the learner's ability to perform the desired behavioral outcomes.
- The change in scope comes from a stakeholder or SME.

It might indicate a mindset of embracing change (and therefore "good") if:
- The underlying nature of or need for the project is changing.
- The content or subject being taught is changing (for example, you're teaching about software and it's the software that's changing).
- The change is the result of an iteration review with learners.

Just because you deem something to be scope creep doesn't automatically mean you don't do it! Sometimes you need to accept this sort of change and do it to satisfy a sponsor or SME's organizational political needs. And that's just fine. As a project manager your role is to keep the team's morale positive throughout because this sort of scope creep can be particularly frustrating.

## This May Be the End of Your Project

Recall that earlier in this chapter I said that this may be the most important hour spent of the entire project. In nearly every instance, the process of defining the goal provides great value to the organization simply by allowing them to understand their needs and their people better. I have found that everyone walks out of this session feeling they have received value from the training team before they even got started creating any deliverables. It can be incredibly uplifting.

It also means that sometimes this discussion uncovers the fact that this project should not proceed. It may be that the goal cannot be met through better training, period, or it may be that the organization cannot even define a goal for this and therefore should put the project on pause.

For example, I was kicking off a project once with a client who wanted training for their salespeople on how to create a value proposition. The kick-off meeting involved the senior vice president for marketing, the senior vice president for sales, and the sales leaders of each of the business units. Around the table were eight people. To start the process of defining this goal, I asked, "What does it mean for a salesperson to create a value proposition?"

As they went around the table, there were seven different definitions of value proposition, and the eighth person said that they did not think that value proposition was something the salesperson should define. We stopped the training project right then and there, saving the business a ton of money, saving all their salespeople from taking training that wasn't aligned with their (clearly nonexistent) business goal, and saving our project team from what would have been a difficult project to complete to anyone's satisfaction.

## What Could Possibly Go Wrong?

Common issues with goal definition include:

**The group spends too much attention on wordsmithing the goal.** If you realize that everyone is spending way too much time arguing about words that don't seem like they make a material difference to the outcome of the project, suggest a pause in the action and consider deferring the details to a future meeting.

**The group leaves key concepts too vague to be meaningful.** Be on the lookout for vague terms to ensure that the group has given you enough definition around them to be able to work with. For example, how is "new hire" defined? How is "speed to performance" defined? What do you mean by "better"? And how do you measure it?

# Key Takeaways

- The goal is never to create training. The goal is to improve performance, and training may be among the deliverables that you use to meet that goal. When you start with the performance outcome–focused goal, the project's scope can be more appropriately defined.
- Ask "Why aren't they doing it now?" This question helps you understand the broader context for the performance goal.
- Define a goal at about 80 percent completeness to keep the kickoff efficient and to signal your openness to change.

# CHAPTER 4

# Define the Learner

**In This Chapter**
- Why use learner personas to create training?
- How do you create learner personas?
- How do you use learner personas in design and development?

For one project, my team and I were asked to create a compliance course on records management—the policies concerning keeping or destroying certain business documents—for a chemicals manufacturer. The two main populations in this company were people who work in an office setting (such as HR, sales, legal, and finance) and people who work in the actual chemical plants themselves. These populations share some basic requirements around records retention, but the types of documents tend to be different. Everyone works on a computer some or all of their time on the job.

This was a new company made up of components of an older, more established company. The people in the plants came from the legacy company, an organization with a very mature record-keeping process. And these people had very low turnover. The personnel in the office are fresh to the new company; most of them were hired within the last three years, and some of them didn't even have a background in the industry.

Records retention is important but different for these two audiences, yet the same course was to cover everyone in the company. I asked if maybe this should be two courses after all: one for plant people, one for office people. No, the client said they only had budget for one course. But a combined course felt like it would lack focus.

Then we asked this most critical question: If this training fails, who is most at risk? The client knew at once that it was the office personnel who were most at risk. They were the ones who didn't have the knowledge, habits, or culture around appropriate records management. Even if the project failed, the personnel in the plant would be able to comply with the records management process without the training—they were doing it today. The office personnel would not be able to do so.

In the end, while everyone had to take the same course, we defined our primary learner as someone from the office personnel. In fact, we brought him to life: His name is Hans. He's a finance employee from Germany, in his late 20s, and has been with the company since it was formed three years

ago. This is his first "real job" after college, although he might not stay with the company for long. He's eager to take online training because he sees it as efficient. Meanwhile, the plant personnel would take this short and simple version of the course, along with following the rest of the regulations they already know.

In this chapter, we'll look at the importance of defining your primary learner and how to create a rich, useful persona that can guide your training development.

# Why Use Learner Personas?

One of the most important ways the project kickoff sets up the project team for success is by helping you—and everyone in the room—define the scope. Scope is the sum of many parts, and, for an instructional design project, understanding the learner is a critical part of defining it. This makes sense. The learner is the final consumer; deliverables that don't address the learners' needs are destined for rework, misuse of resources, and a dubious success rate. Designing for the right learner will keep the project on track because resources will be focused in the right direction.

You might already be familiar with learner personas or the idea behind them. Marketers often call them empathy maps and software designers use the term user stories, but the idea is pretty much the same: understanding the target consumers' routines, pain points, needs, aspirations, and prior knowledge or comfort with what will be delivered to them. Personas are a key part of design thinking and user-centered design as well. The similarities in goals means that your project team could borrow tools from marketing or software design to help you understand your learners; many instructional designers have done that successfully. However, using the learner persona template and the accompanying process in this chapter to describe and select learner personas is especially well-suited to learning and development projects.

Learner personas are powerful tools throughout a project's timeline, from kickoff to going live. The process of developing learner personas is often an eye-opening experience for project sponsors and stakeholders during the kickoff. For many, this is the first time they've been asked to consider what the learners need and whether training is actually the right solution for the problem. And even when all agree that training is the right solution, the solution that sponsors and stakeholders originally envisioned can change significantly as they develop learner personas. Suddenly, the mobile app that delivers just-in-time performance support becomes less viable when decision makers realize that learners who operate equipment almost constantly throughout their shifts have little time to dig a phone out of their pockets to pull up an app. Or, the vision for one comprehensive course module evolves to an experience consisting of several shorter modules, which can better accommodate learners (such as truck drivers or flight crews) whose shift lengths are regulated by external governance and whose learning must be brief enough to fit into that limited time frame.

During the instructional design and training development phase, the learner persona influences all manner of decisions. Some of the ways learner personas affect the design are expected, such as who's depicted in the visuals (younger or older, dressed casually or formally, and so on) and the types of activities and post-course follow-up that is provided, while other ways in which the persona will affect decisions can't be predicted.

For example, in a course about basic finance for entrepreneurs my team helped develop, our SME was a PhD student and researcher in business finance—supremely qualified to be the SME! We decided the course's primary learner persona aspired to be the CEO of a manufacturing company with $30 million in annual revenue. The SME fully expected to provide the standard business school finance material, which includes heavy emphasis on bond and stock markets as funding choices for business decision makers. However, these funding choices are not options for small manufacturing companies, and we left this material out of an early draft with a request for replacement content. After reconfirming the primary learner persona with the project sponsor, the module on financing options instead included sections on organic growth, bank loans, angel investment and loans, vendor financing, and other options that were more attainable for smaller businesses. Much more appropriate!

## How to Develop Learner Personas

Agile projects focus on the end users—the learners—who are generally not at all like the project sponsor requesting the project or the project team working to design it. This means that the project team and the project sponsor must set aside assumptions about what learners want and focus instead on what they actually need. This starts with developing detailed, rich learner personas.

To be effective, you need to create personas that are believable as real people. They need names, biographical profiles, and photos that could truly represent a learner in your target audience. Each learner persona should be fleshed out with interests, motivations, recreational activities, professional goals, and level of comfort with technology (particularly useful for e-learning and digital projects). While it's possible to model a persona on an actual person, I do not advise this. The persona should amalgamate traits that a group of targeted learners share.

Typically, the vast majority of learners in a given project can be defined in three to five personas. For instance, you might have a group of learners who are new hires, and a second group who have been on the job for several years. These groups' needs are different and could result in two personas. One persona, representing the experienced workers, might be refreshing her knowledge and learning what's changed in the regulations, while the other, the new hire, needs more detail and foundational information. Personas could be defined around people who are eager to learn and perform well and those who are no longer engaged in their role. Or, geography or demographics may be the differentiator among personas.

During the analysis and discussion of personas, the question of stereotyping is likely to arise. While personas are certainly generalizations about learners—inferences based on careful observation and personal experiences—they are not stereotypes. A stereotype is a list of traits, beliefs, or behaviors that one assumes apply to all members of a group whereas generalizations describe a group based on its typical members. Think of personas as archetypes, not stereotypes. A key difference in creating personas is that in defining more than one persona, the project team is acknowledging that the learner population is made up of diverse individuals who cannot be characterized by a single "stereotypical" learner, but can be broadly described by a few representative groups.

Over the years I've used several approaches to defining personas, and I share them here in the hope that one or more of them makes sense for your work. Figure 4-1 offers some questions you could ask and answer when defining each persona (the full list appears in the appendix). I typically draw from this list when I am leading the kickoff group to define personas, but using all the questions is by no means required (or even useful). Alternatively, Figure 4-2 is a poster I use to let kickoff session members create their own personas.

**Figure 4-1.** Sample Learner Persona Questions

**Demographics**
- What is his/her name?
- What is his/her age?
- What is his/her gender?
- What is his/her primary language?

**Professional Demographics**
- What company does s/he work for?
- What is his/her job title?
- How long has s/he been with the company?
- How long has s/he been in their current position?

**Connection to the Learning and Learning Approaches**
- What has motivated s/he to take the course?
- How often will s/he apply what they learn in the course?
- Has s/he taken training courses before?
- What type of computer does s/he typically use?

**Away From Work**
- How does s/he use social media?
- What does s/he like to do during spare time?
- What was the last book s/he read?
- What car does s/he drive?

**Figure 4-2.** Learner Persona Template

# LEARNER/USER PERSONA

Lot Like Agile Management Approach™ | LLAMA | © TorranceLearning

Regardless of the tools you use to create personas, the high level of detail makes the personas seem more like real people, which makes them relatable. Designers and developers can imagine these fictitious individuals using the course, experiencing successes and frustrations—which helps them design and provide the best possible learner experience. Consider the example in Figure 4-3.

**Figure 4-3.** Learner Persona Example

---

**Name:** Geoffrey

**Age:** 42

Geoff has spent the last five years of his career as a project manager in the IT department and aspires to someday become the director of IT. Prior to working at his current company, he held IT positions at several small to mid-size companies throughout the Northeast. While he feels comfortable in his current role and enjoys the sense of power he has over his six direct reports, he knows that to move forward in his career he will need to keep his tools and techniques on the cutting edge. He wants to look smart and competent.

Geoff puts in 45-50 hours a week plus driving 45 minutes to get to the office each day, meaning that his wife Karen does most of the chauffeuring of their two kids, Alex (10) and Bethany (eight), to their various extracurricular activities. On the weekends when he's not at work, Geoff spends most of his time doing work around the house. If he's lucky, he'll have time to check on his fantasy football team, but usually he gives up after a few weeks and lets the roster sit through the end of the season, leaving it up to luck and good fortune to determine whether he wins the pool of money that his he and his college buddies contributed. This is an approach he often falls back on with his work projects, too.

Geoff likes it when he has the opportunity to complete his required training and development activities via e-learning because it means that he can go at his own pace and fit it into his busy schedule wherever time allows. Even better is when he can watch and learn via his shiny new tablet since he almost always has it with him, often while watching TV.

---

In your kickoff meeting, you can use flip charts, whiteboards, or worksheets with a column for each learner persona. After describing the end result—the learning and performance goals—at a high level, you start defining the learner personas. The questions provided in Figure 4-1 can provide more detail, allowing the team to work toward a consensus-based definition. Rough out a learner's persona before moving on to the next learner. You'll often come up with new questions as you work. Feel free to go back and answer these new questions for all the previously defined learners so you have comparable descriptions.

## Defining the Primary Learner Persona

For most projects, you'll probably define somewhere between three and five personas. From those, you'll identify the primary learner persona (PLP). It's not unusual for a project sponsor to balk at defining just one primary persona; "everyone will need to take this course!" the sponsor will shout. While perhaps this is true, you can't meet everyone's needs all the time, and it's therefore critical to know whose needs you must meet. While everyone in the target audience will be expected to take the course, the PLP represents the most critical segment of that audience to reach.

By defining the PLP, you create better training, and you manage scope. You create better training because the entire course is coherent around a specific set of needs. You manage scope by having a built-in filter against which to evaluate each new idea that comes up: Does this make the experience for the PLP better? If not, this is an easy one to set aside for later. If so, then you have the additional questions around impacts to the timeline and resources, but at least you've validated that this is a sensible change to the project.

In some cases, defining the PLP is an easy task; it is obvious to all. On some projects, though, deciding which persona is the PLP is the toughest decision of the kickoff process. These discussions, as well as various stakeholders' arguments for or against each persona, provide tremendous insight into the learners' needs, pain points, and goals.

How the choice of primary persona is made varies from project to project. Here are a few examples from actual projects (Torrance 2014):

- In a concussion education course for coaches, the client chose the high school football coach persona over the girls soccer coach and the recreational flag football coach personas. The client's public health educators felt that a school's sports culture and attitudes around concussion were led by the football program. Messages aimed at the football coach would be accepted by other coaches but perhaps not vice versa.

- In a supervisory skills class for a food manufacturing company, the client felt that 50 percent of the learner population would be eager to learn more and improve their skills. The other 50 percent would be dismissive of these "soft skills." Since the class would be taught in five quarterly sessions, the client wanted to be sure that supervisors would continue to come to all the sessions. The skeptical learner was chosen as the PLP because getting them to apply the skills and come back for more training was the biggest challenge the project faced.

## Using Learner Personas in Design and Development

The personas are for your team's use—the learners don't ever need to know that they exist! The goal in using a PLP is to design learning that meets the described learner's needs—as well as the needs of other learners. It is not meant to exclude learners or tailor content narrowly for only a subset of learners.

Making the PLP seem like a real, relatable person helps the project team and sponsors stay focused on learners' needs and experience. Instructional designers can easily get caught up in details of the screen layout and navigation, technology, and compatibility with other parts of the sponsor's learning ecosystem, SMEs' insistence on including every detail of content that might possibly be relevant, and much more. The PLP has specific goals and needs, and, when faced with requests to add more features or content, the project team can point out that these details or features are outside of the scope since the PLP doesn't need them. In this way, the PLP both guides the instructional designers' work and provides a clear rationale for decisions on content or features. This helps the team avoid scope creep, and ensures that the final product will meet real learners' needs.

Choosing a single PLP helps in another way as well: It avoids the one-size-fits-all approach to learning. A single product cannot and should not be all things to all learners. Focusing on the PLP avoids that trap, resulting in more effective training.

Once you've created your learner personas, you can further refine your project and avoid scope creep by developing user stories.

## What Could Possibly Go Wrong?

Common issues with learner personas include:

**You confuse learner personas for job roles.** While learners with different jobs or different levels of experience may well have different needs—and could even become different personas—the job role may not be the only or even the most salient consideration in developing a persona. Two people in similar roles might have different pain points, levels of comfort with technology, and approaches to using the training you create. Learners in a variety of user roles could have similar goals in completing the training—learning how regulations have changed, for example, or mastering a new piece of software.

**Learner personas rely too heavily on demographic stereotypes.** Not all Millennial employees will expect the same thing out of learning, nor are they interchangeable in terms of their comfort with technology, preference for consuming training or e-learning at work or on the go, or any other aspect of the learner persona that might guide instructional design. While sensitivity to the different needs and preferences of members of various ages, genders, or other demographic groups is recommended, a persona's focus on a single individual helps project teams avoid designing for a clichéd stereotype of a group—and remain focused on specific learners' needs and experiences.

**You force too much precision on the learner personas.** Personas can grow and change. Remember that this is an Agile development approach—it's iterative. As your team works through iterations and gets feedback, the personas might evolve to accurately reflect the experience of testers using the prototypes. That's not only OK, it's encouraged! Remember: Accept and expect change.

## Key Takeaways

- Learner personas help you understand the learner population as real people with needs, motivations, and aspirations relative to your project.
- The primary learner persona is a critical piece of defining project scope for an Agile project, and serves as a built-in decision criterion when faced with the inevitable future suggestions to add or change something on the project: Does this improve the performance of the primary learner persona?
- The learner personas then help the project team connect with learners throughout the design and development process, as well as provide a definition for suggested reviewers for future iterations.

# CHAPTER 5

# Define Scope With User Stories

In This Chapter
- How do we define scope in terms of modular pieces?
- How does scope definition support Agile?
- How do user stories work in L&D?

My team and I were kicking off a project that was part of a curriculum to teach basic concepts of capitalism to small business owners in formerly communist countries where financial acumen in business was lacking. As the professor (who was both the SME and a co-sponsor of the project) was talking about what he envisioned as the project's scope, I pulled out my 3x5 cards and started writing my notes in the form of user stories. As he moved from big topic to big topic, I started piling the cards in groups.

All of a sudden he paused, then reached across the table and started rearranging the cards into an order that made better sense for the course, including moving a set of cards way off to the side. "These are things I don't want in the course, I was just telling you about them for context." In this simple exercise we had arrived at a shared vision for the project's scope, with a clear definition of what was not to be covered.

When I ask instructional designers and developers what makes the best kind of project experience, "a shared definition of scope" is the number 1 thing that's mentioned over and over. Oftentimes when a learning project is commissioned, the project sponsor is asking for a course on "value proposition" or "forklift driver safety," and they may even have a set of intended course objectives, but that's still a pretty vague sense of scope. Here in the kickoff session, now that we know the goal of the project and who the learners are (including the primary learner), we're ready to define the scope at a much more practical and actionable level.

A software team using Agile will define scope in units known as user stories. This is an incredibly useful approach for building software (we'll talk about this in a minute) but is lacking in one key area that concerns us in the L&D field: performance objectives. After struggling with a user stories–only approach to Agile for a few years, my team and I discovered Cathy Moore's Action Mapping approach. Action Mapping was created to support excellent instructional design—and it does that well—but we also found added benefits in terms of scope definition to support project management.

The user stories technique offers the L&D team some benefits, so we'll cover that topic in this chapter, then Cathy Moore's Action Mapping in chapter 6. Both methods are well-documented in other forms (such as Mountain Goat Software for user stories and Moore's 2017 book, *Map It!*

*The Hands-On Guide to Strategic Training Design*) so these chapters will provide enough of an overview to get you started, along with the specifics that are essential to support the LLAMA approach.

Please note: For projects where you are defining requirements for learning platforms, apps, and physical spaces—deliverables that *do* something, perform a task, and so on—scope is defined by writing user stories as outlined in this chapter.

## User Stories

User stories are the smallest units of scope in an Agile project. Given Agile's emphasis on delivering value to the customer, they are written in terms of the end user's goal for using the software, and they're expressed in nontechnical terms. The needs of a variety of end users can be prioritized, sorted, and used as the scope definition for a unit of work, sprint, or iteration for an Agile team.

In a software project, user stores are similar and related to—but not the same as—system requirements. System requirements are typically not written from the end user's perspective and may contain elements that are completely invisible or even irrelevant to end users.

The format of a user story is key to this user-centric approach. It goes like this:

*As a <who> I want <what> so I can/because <why>.*

Using this template forces the team to think about what the users want (and you could even ask them!), and it encourages thinking about the needs of a wide variety of user types. Often the "who" in the statement above is one of the learner personas, with the primary persona often having the most user stories. Other roles also have needs and stories, such as the LMS administrator or a legal compliance team. This allows the team to define a rich picture of needs from which scope can be defined.

User stories are traditionally documented on 3x5 index cards, one story per card. This is an incredibly useful technique for several reasons:

- It's democratic and participative—anyone can write a card. The kickoff session is where many of them get written, although they can be added at any point.
- Cards can be easily discarded (ideally recycled) in favor of better ideas.
- Cards can be easily grouped and sorted just by moving them around.
- Modern Agile project management software tools continue the theme of a single "card" per user story, although they lose out on the tactile nature of the index cards. You might consider using the physical cards for user story generation workshops, then transcribing them to your online tools later on.

## Getting the "Right" Size

It's not unusual for stories to be written at a high level—too broad to be useful. What is typically needed is to drill down to more detail on a user story, either by adding conditions and details to it or by breaking it into smaller stories. For example, the following user story probably needs a bit more detail:

As a learning leader, I want to see a dashboard with analytics about training so I can see what people are doing in the learning ecosystem.

How will you know it needs more detail? Well, I suspect that if that's all the team delivered, I'd be unsatisfied with it. For example, the team might deliver a dashboard, but because the user story was so vague, the final product doesn't include all the analytics the learning leader needs, or they might not be presented in a way that's best designed for her specific reporting requirements. Mike Cohn of Mountain Goat Software says, "User stories are part of an Agile approach that helps shift the focus from writing about requirements to talking about them. All Agile user stories include a written sentence or two and, more importantly, a series of conversations about the desired functionality. . . . In fact, these discussions are more important than whatever text is written" (Cohn n.d.)

(An added bonus about Mike Cohn's website is that he is a trainer of Agile, so many of his examples have to do with creating a training product. This makes many of his examples inherently relevant to the work that we do as instructional designers.)

By asking a series of questions like "what do you mean by XXX," "what happens if YYY," and "what would you do with ZZZ," you can solicit the additional detail you need to sufficiently define a story. Asking more about our example above, we might derive sub-stories such as:

- As a learning leader, I want to specify an audience group on a dashboard so I can narrow down my review of their activity.
- As a learning leader, I want to specify a date range on a dashboard so I can narrow down my review of their activity.
- As a learning leader, I want to specify a course or curriculum on a dashboard so I can look across all activity for a particular topic.
- As an LMS administrator, I want to create multiple custom dashboards so each team or leader can see the data they are most interested in.
- As an LMS administrator, I want to copy a custom dashboard so I get a fast start on creating new versions.
- As an LMS administrator, I want to delete a custom dashboard so my failed attempts or things we don't use any longer don't clutter my list of currently active dashboards.
- As a learning leader, I want to print my dashboard to PDF so I can save it or email it to others.
- As a learning leader, I want to send a link to my dashboard to others.

- As a learning leader, I want to see activity from both inside and outside the LMS on my dashboard because I know that learning doesn't only happen inside the LMS.

Did you notice something? None of the story examples tells you anything about how it will be accomplished. The user story doesn't define a feature or specify a solution. It simply outlines the user's goal and leaves it to the team's own creative process to determine how best to meet that goal.

## Using User Stories in L&D Projects

If the Agile user stories technique isn't useful for designing learning experiences, why bother describing it in a book about LLAMA? First, I consider it important to have an appreciation for what software teams are doing with Agile so that you understand how what you're doing is different. It would be a confusing conversation if you and a more traditional Agile practitioner were to get together to talk about defining scope only to realize that the LLAMA approach varies in this particular aspect.

Second, and perhaps more importantly, instructional designers and project managers do much more than design course content. L&D teams can use the user stories technique to define scope for a variety of project types. Check out the examples in Table 5-1.

**Table 5-1.** Sample User Stories

| Project Type | Sample User Stories |
|---|---|
| Designing performance support | As a customer intake specialist, I want a reminder of the key steps that I need to follow within easy view, so I can refer to it. |
| | As a customer intake specialist, I want a list of definitions for less frequently used fields, so I can be sure I'm correctly coding things without losing speed when I'm with a customer. |
| | As a support analyst, I want to see what documents in the support system are being used versus not, so I can learn more about the needs of the intake specialists. |

| Specifying needs for an LMS or other learning software | As an employee, I want to know what I need to do and when it's due, so I can get it done without being nagged by my manager.<br><br>As a manager, I want to know who is late on their required training, so I can nag them to complete it.<br><br>As an LMS administrator, I want to see how many people are in the audience I define for a course, so I can make a quick check to see if I've got the right group. |
|---|---|
| Designing a classroom environment | As an instructor, I want to project my screen in the room from any device (Apple, PC, iOS phone, Android phone, tablets), so I can just bring whatever I have to class.<br><br>As an instructor, I want to have access to smaller breakout rooms so activities can be done privately and not within earshot of other teams.<br><br>As a participant, I want to have a coffee station nearby, so I can quickly get a beverage whenever I need and not miss too much class time. |
| Event planning, such as a workshop or a conference | As a paid participant, I want to review sessions, times, and descriptions in advance of arrival, so I can create a schedule.<br><br>As a paid participant, I want to be able to get a refund if I cancel or change my plans, so I can get my money back.<br><br>As a conference speaker, I want to know how many people to expect in my session, so I can bring the right number of handouts. |
| The features and options for an e-learning course | As a learner, I want to download all the course materials without having to launch the e-learning course.<br><br>As a learner, I want to search the course for a specific topic, so I can skip to a concept I want to learn more about.<br><br>As a learning engineer, I want the course to send learner activity via xAPI, so I can use my LRS to analyze the experience. |

In fact, user stories can be a helpful technique for designing just about anything except the actual learning experience itself, for which Cathy Moore's Action Mapping approach is far more effective.

When you're in the kickoff session, you might feel frustrated by the process of writing these stories, overwhelmed by the amount of information at your disposal, or stumped by where to begin. Here are some tips for user story sessions (some of which were first published in my 2014 *TD at Work*, "Agile and LLAMA for ISD Project Management"):

- Generate more ideas than you think you'll need. Often the best ideas come after the team has an opportunity to reflect, add to, and combine other ideas. Later on you'll have the opportunity to choose the ones that are most meaningful to the project.

- Like most brainstorming and idea generation exercises, save the evaluation of ideas for a subsequent step. You may want to highlight controversial ideas or things that will need further exploration so you can come back to them later.

- Use techniques that help you get contributions from everyone in the room. A period of silent brainstorming or "brainwriting" gives quiet or shy people the opportunity to express their ideas.

- Accept ideas from everyone. With Agile, everyone can write a story.

- Photograph whatever you come up with before you leave the room. In addition to providing a sharable record of the session, the spatial memory and layout of the results may later trigger memories and associations.

- Challenge participants to define a meaningful "why" for each card. A card without a "why" may have low priority or may not be necessary at all.

- A card with a "why" that sounds something like, "Because everyone will need to know this!" should be a red flag to you as the instructional designer.

## Sorting User Stories

Once you have your user stories, you can sort them for a variety of purposes. The first and foremost would be to define scope for the project, either as "in scope" or "out of scope," in terms of priority order as "must have" vs. "nice to have," or in phases. Sometimes this is defined by level of finish, sometimes by user, sometimes by phase or timeline, and so on. Whichever way you do it is fine so long as the end goal is a definition of scope that's shared among the project sponsor, the SME, and the project team. Stories may be grouped into larger "epics" or phases of work.

If you find yourself wavering over a user story, unable to sort it into an in-scope pile or an out-of-scope pile, you may need to break that story down into sub-stories to sort.

User stories that are determined to be lower priority or for future phases often do not get defined at a more detailed level until a time closer to when they will be worked on. That way you're not expending effort to define something that may continually get pushed to a lower priority or never even done.

The key shortcoming of the user story method is that, while it is an excellent technique for documenting functions and features, I've found that attempts to account for learning objectives and performance outcomes are a stretch. Our team struggled with this for several years until we discovered Cathy Moore's Action Mapping approach to instructional design, which we'll cover in the next chapter.

## What Could Possibly Go Wrong?

Common issues with user stories include:

**You use this technique alone on an instructional project.** The user story technique does not capture the course objectives well and therefore might not always meet your needs for a scope-defining mechanism.

**You get too detailed too early.** Things will inevitably change or evolve as the project unfolds, so don't waste your time getting too detailed on user stories that won't be needed until much later.

## Key Takeaways

- User stories are the most granular unit of scope in an Agile project.
- User stories work well for software and "things that do something" like a classroom or app, but not for instructional content.
- User stories need to be defined at a sufficient level of detail in order to be meaningful.
- User stories can be sorted into "in scope" and "out of scope" activities and thus create a shared definition of project scope.

# CHAPTER 6

# Define Scope Using Action Mapping

## In This Chapter

- How does Action Mapping lend itself to scope definition?
- Why should you break up the goal into behaviors?
- When should you introduce content to your plan?

Very early in my career, I had my "dream project" (or so I thought then). The client had been hiring a Harvard Business School professor to teach an in-person class to new marketing professionals on a regular basis. The client found that this was an expensive way to teach these foundational topics—flying in people from around the world, hiring the professor each time—and it meant that the marketers needed to wait until the next class offering to learn the material. If the class was only taught annually or semi-annually, this could be a long wait. As such, the client wanted to convert this instructor-led training to an e-learning course, then bring in the professor for an advanced course taught less frequently and to only a select group of learners. The client would pay the professor to license the content and pay me to create e-learning on it.

In order to absorb the content for the course, the professor and I met at a mutually convenient airport hotel conference room, and I got a private, four-hour lecture on a topic I happened to find fascinating. He was an excellent teacher—a really engaging guy—and I loved every minute of it. At the end of the lecture, he handed me his book and said, "The client wants chapters 1-6 in their own corporate language." Easy enough!

I had my charge and I was off and running. I spent the next month writing and designing the course and really enjoying myself. Aside from a review of the storyboard, I never spoke with the professor again.

The trouble is I have no idea to this day how that content was applied on the job. Like any solid instructional designer, it was easy enough to derive what appeared to be meaningful course objectives (and, incredibly, there was a chapter on each one!). And it was pretty clear to me how to create engaging interactions with the content. It was a very content-centric course. The client loved it and by all reports, the learners did too. But any connection to an on-the-job behavior would have been purely coincidental.

This course is on my bucket list of courses I would love to have the opportunity to do over.

The traditional Agile user story approach breaks down, or is at least rather cumbersome, in the instructional design process where we have a specific behavioral objective—something that I'm sure the course I just described could really have used. Using traditional Agile user stories for training projects tends to result in very information-driven courses to the great frustration of the instructional design team and, ultimately, the learner. This leads us to an essential deviation from the traditional Agile process that we use in the LLAMA approach: Cathy Moore's Action Mapping process, the means by which we generate stories for our project estimating and planning.

This chapter will give you a high-level overview of the process with the goal of using it to then define scope as the step analogous to user stories in an Agile process. I recommend you read Moore's book *Map It!* (2017) for a deeper look at Action Mapping. Note that Moore's method is not intended as a project management tool. I have found that its granular approach to breaking down performance needs lends itself just as well to scope definition as traditional Agile's user stories. In this way, we get a double lift for this method: great instructional design and scope management for our project.

## Starting the Action Map

Action Mapping begins with the goal definition that was covered in chapter 3, ideally in response to a specific problem the organization needs to solve. During the kickoff session with project stakeholders, SMEs, and the instructional design team, you will identify the actions that the primary learner persona (PLP) from chapter 4 will take when successfully attaining the business goal (Figure 6-1). This is one area where the project management method supports excellence in instructional design: When actions are visible and measurable behaviors, you create the framework for a results-focused and interesting course.

You'll need a large space for your action mapping—a whiteboard, wall, or screen that everyone can see. Start by writing the goal you defined in the middle of the space. Then as the group identifies the behaviors, write them around the goal as shown in Figure 6-1. Sometimes these are in order, like steps to be followed, and sometimes they can be grouped into categories.

Figure 6-1 offers sample behaviors around a goal, drawn from several different courses to show both hard skills and soft skills can be action mapped.

**Figure 6-1.** What Behaviors Align With Your Goal?

## Defining Scope in Terms of Behavioral Outcomes

At this point in the project kickoff, you're still in the realm of performance consulting with the project sponsor and the SMEs. You haven't begun any work on the instructional design of the deliverables.

It's an excellent time to review the actions you've identified and start doing some basic scoping for the project. Are there actions that can be grouped together as similar skills? Which actions are expected of beginners and which are more suitable for experts? Are there actions that are already supported in other courses? Which ones are tied to decisions that will be made in the near future, for which we should hold off building training right now (if we can)? Is there any debate about the nature or importance of any of these? Why don't people perform this properly already? Is it possible that training is not the answer? One foundation to successful scope definition is to know what not to do, and action mapping at this stage of the process is an excellent place to start laying that out.

And, much like Agile user stories, you will often have behaviors that need to be broken down into sub-behaviors to be meaningful. For example, if you were operating a roofing company, one behavior for your technicians, "Nail roof shingles safely," could be broken down into the following sub-behaviors:

1. Put on and secure appropriate fall protection gear.
2. Nail the aluminum drip edge flush with the edge of the roof.
3. Snap a chalk line to get a straight edge.
4. Lay out and nail down roofing felt paper.
5. Mark the roof for the first course of shingles.
6. Install a starter course by cutting off the three tabs on a shingle, leaving only the top tar section.

These sub-behaviors may result in a more meaningful level of detail for scope definition conversations. For the course above, you may decide that you need to teach how to measure and mark the roof, or you may discover that you have already covered it in a course elsewhere that just needs some tuning. The Action Mapping process sparks these conversations and thus helps the design team, the project sponsor, SMEs, and the stakeholders establish a shared vision for scope.

## Brainstorming Practice Opportunities

Here's where the instructional design comes in: For each behavior, you will identify ways in which learners can practice or interact with the content in some meaningful fashion. Generate a few ideas for each one so that you can choose the best modality for the situation, scoping the project's size, timeline, and budget as you select media and approaches. Generally these practice activities are laid out as they are shown in Figure 6-2.

**Figure 6-2.** How Can the Learner Practice the Behavior?

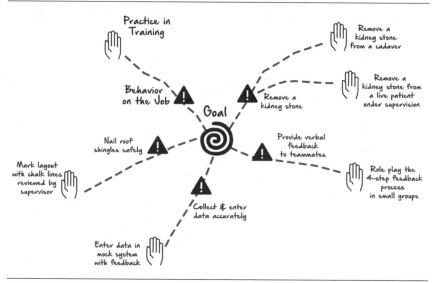

This step of the action mapping process may take place in the kickoff meeting, or it may take place afterward when the instructional design team has an opportunity to work together on it. Including the stakeholders and SMEs in this part of the exercise has its benefits. The action map, together with the primary learner persona, helps everyone understand the scope of the project and the level of proficiency the learners need to attain to meet the business goal. Thus the practice activities become a logical next step for the group.

In other cases, I've found that this instructional design work is best done by the project team with options to be presented to the project sponsor at a subsequent meeting. This allows the instructional design team more time to gather ideas before presenting an approach for the course, and it focuses the time and efforts of the non-instructional-designer members of the kickoff session on the information they are most uniquely qualified to provide.

## Identifying Content to Support Practice Activities

The final component of the action map is the information needed to complete the practice activities. Instead of merely converting old slide decks and instructor guides into the new course, the only information requested from SMEs and sponsors is directly related to the project at hand. It also keeps the information in the course focused on the actions the learner needs to take on the job. This will guide you to more focused, effective, and probably more interesting training.

The practice activities in the course may support multiple actions, just as a single action may have multiple practice opportunities in the course, as shown in Figure 6-3. A one-to-one relationship does not need to be maintained. Similarly, the knowledge required for the course does not have to be in a one-to-one relationship with the practice opportunities.

**Figure 6-3.** What Content Do You Need to Support Practice?

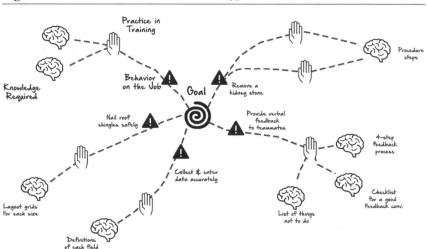

# Action Mapping as a Scope-Defining Tool

The project work of the instructional design team is to define, develop, and present the practice activities and supporting knowledge and information in a meaningful way in the course. Each practice activity and each piece of content or knowledge serves essentially the same role in scope definition as the Agile user story.

You could almost go so far as to write them as user stories (although you wouldn't need to do it unless you were also integrating your stories with those of an Agile software team—see chapter 10) like this:

- As a first-time team leader, I role-play the four-step feedback process in the classroom, so I can feel comfortable using it to give verbal feedback to teammates.

- As a first-time team leader, I want to review the four-step feedback process, so I can use it to give verbal feedback to teammates.

- As a surgery resident, I remove a kidney stone from a cadaver, so I can prepare to remove a kidney stone from a real patient.

- As a surgery resident, I want to review the generally accepted procedure for removing a kidney stone, so I can make the most of my cadaver time.

- As a new hire at Acme Roofing, I mark my chalk lines and have them reviewed by my supervisor before nailing, so I have some confirmation I'm doing it right.

- As a new hire at Acme Roofing, I want to refer to common shingle layout grids, so I can nail roof shingles accurately without redoing the math all the time.

Most instructional projects will have several traditional user stories in addition to the action map. Those user stories meet additional user needs that aren't adequately captured by the action map, such as enrollment and certificate needs, LMS interactions, and so on.

You've defined the project's goal and narrowed the project's scope through personas, user stories, and action mapping, and it's time to wrap up the project kickoff. Chapters 2-6 should help you ensure you're getting the project off on the right foot while remaining flexible for the inevitable but still unexpected changes. Let's now turn our focus to the job of managing an iterative Agile project.

## What Could Possibly Go Wrong?

Common issues with action mapping in scope definition include:

**You don't do the action map.** Even if the request for your project team is to simply give an existing course a facelift, I strongly recommend this as an opportunity to do an action mapping exercise, however abbreviated, to confirm that this course and this content in this approach is still meaningful.

**You do too much action mapping during the kickoff session.** Typically, you will get through the goal and the behaviors and sketch out some practice and some knowledge where relevant. It's okay to leave the rest of the details to a future session with a smaller group of SMEs and instructional designers.

**You start with the content and try to action map from it.** As I like to say in my workshops, any instructional designer worth their salt can make interesting interactive training from the phone book. A content-first strategy will tend to result in bloated information dumps. Action mapping keeps your instructional work focused on practical behavioral outcomes.

## Key Takeaways

- Cathy Moore's Action Mapping technique is an excellent instructional design approach that happens to lend itself well to an Agile-style scope definition process.
- Start shaping the scope of the project as you determine the behaviors required for successful goal attainment.

- Practice activities can be scoped for size, depth, and quantity as needed.
- By saving content requirements for last, only the information required to meet the desired behaviors and the goal are included in the project.
- The practice activities and knowledge delivery aspects of the action map are analogous to the Agile user story.

# Part 2:
## Managing the Project

# Plan the Iterative Project

**In This Chapter**
- What type of project is this?
- How do you plan from the top down to arrive at a high-level schedule?
- How do you plan from the bottom up to make sure there's enough time and resources to do all the work?
- How can you make plans for the unexpected?
- How can visual tools assist your planning?

In the early days at TorranceLearning, we had a small team, a handful of clients, and only a few relatively simple projects at any given time. Back then it was easy enough to manage our work and keep things in our heads, a few Excel sheets, and email threads. As we grew, added teammates, and had a larger client base and more complex projects, it became clear that this ad hoc method of managing our work was not going to be scalable. This was also about the same time that we began adopting Agile, so the visual planning inherent in the Agile process was quite welcome by the team.

Of course, being a digitally focused company, I initially turned up my nose at the paper and corkboard–based model taught by most Agile practitioners at the time. Plus, we had just installed our first professional

network file server and I was more than happy to use it.

I created an Excel sheet that contained all our projects and all the weeks of the year. For each project, I entered the phase or iteration it was planned to be in for each week, and the people assigned to each phase. With the magic of Excel's conditional formatting, the sheet automatically highlighted situations in which team members were over- or under-allocated. I saved this beauty of a spreadsheet on the network where everyone could have access to it. How transparent of me!

And promptly, everyone pretty much ignored the sheet, including me . . .

. . . until there was a crisis . . .

. . . and then the sheet would be too out of date to inform us of anything.

Clearly this was not a useful tool for us. It was visual and color coded, but not out front where it needed to be.

Since then we've been through two major iterations of our project planning methods, and many, many small tweaks have been made along the way to fine-tune things. We find that keeping our high-level planning tools visual, tactile, and front-and-center is critical to making sure that our decisions are well-informed.

Each team will settle on a group of tools and processes that fit for you, your organization, and your work. Don't be afraid to experiment—use Agile to implement this! Let's dive in.

With the scope defined, the project sponsor's timeline and budget in consideration, and the work effort estimated, you are now ready to plan the work. And work! A LLAMA-based project is planned from the top down and the bottom up.

Top-down planning covers the major milestones, start and end dates, and key interactions with other projects. This high-level arc of the project is generally planned in terms of weeks and months, depending on the size of the project. This is the project plan that most stakeholders and the project sponsor will interact with.

The bottom-up plan is based on the tasks and estimates for each iteration, effectively laying out the tasks required to reach the next milestone. This plan is reflected in hours and days and is the one that the project team spends the most time focusing on—the plan to meet each high-level milestone. When the top-down and the bottom-up plans do not meet, that's an opportunity for discussion with the project sponsor.

## Three Types of Projects

Classic project management practice holds that there are three types of projects, and the same applies to Agile and LLAMA. Knowing which type of project you're on is key to being able to plan the project and guides how you will handle the inevitable changes and hiccups as the project progresses. Projects can be categorized by three constraints: time, resources, and scope.

**Projects that are constrained by time.** In this instance, there is a relatively firm due date by which the team needs to complete their deliverables. Training projects constrained by time are often ones that need to release in conjunction with some other effort within the organization or an externally imposed due date. Some examples of time-constrained projects could be:

- training that must be available when a new software system is available in the market

- training to prepare people for an event like a trade show or product release
- compliance training that must be released when new rules and regulations go into effect.

**Projects that are constrained by resources.** Here you face a limited amount of money or people available to complete the project. Training projects constrained by resources must produce their deliverables within the specified budget or with only the available resources. Resource-constrained projects are typically in situations like this:

- grant-funded training with a pre-defined spending cap
- organizations with tightly controlled spending limits and budgets
- governments
- training that must be developed by a specific person or team, with no ability to add staff or outsource the effort.

**Projects that are constrained by scope.** What matters most for these projects is that the training covers the specified content and deliverables, with less (but certainly some) emphasis on the time or resources required to get there. Setting aside (temporarily) considerations about content-driven versus performance-based instructional design, practical considerations about the breadth and depth of training often influence project management. Scope is the most subjectively defined of the three project constraints and gives you the most flexibility in terms of delivery. Scope-constrained projects can be found in situations where:

- Training must cover all functions or features of a product (and sometimes the scope of these may not be known until late in the project for new releases).
- Training cannot take more learner time than specified (such as a regulatory-specified class length or e-learning seat time).
- Training must meet a defined quantity of delivery modes or deliverables.

The project sponsor usually determines before or during the project kickoff session which of the three types of constraints is most central to the project (chapter 3). Often this discussion offers some valuable insight into the project for everyone involved. I've found that even where the answer may seem obvious, asking about constraints sparks some useful conversations. If you make assumptions about a constraint, invariably you will be incorrect some or most of the time. For example, one time my team and I were on a large grant-funded project that we assumed had a hard deliverable date. As it turned out, our client could apply for a timeline extension through the grantor to accommodate some needed additions to scope, although there could be no additional funding.

It is possible that during the course of the project a timebound delivery schedule could become scope-bound when a change important enough to adjust the delivery date comes into play. Or a scope-bound project could become resource-constrained when budget cuts are implemented. The key is to know about the changes as soon as possible and adjust accordingly.

Once you've determined the constraints, and which are the hard and soft ones, that leads into scheduling. You'll want to consider the top-down schedule of major milestones and due dates alongside the detailed bottom-up schedule of individual tasks to be completed. The top-down plan outlines where and when the project will begin and end, and the bottom-up schedule shows how you'll get there (and if you have the time and resources to do so). These two schedules are "living" constructs and evolve together over the duration of the project.

## Top-Down Planning

Top-down project planning creates what I call the high-level arc of the project—the major milestones and due dates, the iterative cycles of reviews, and key inputs and intersections with other projects, along with timeframes when the project will be able to move slower or faster than other times. When you lay out the iterations and review cycles for the project, you'll gain insight into when you'll need time from SMEs, when you'll need reviewers engaged, and so on.

Start with a pro forma project plan for periods of work and periods of review (Figure 7-1). (More about iterative development and review cycles will be covered in chapter 9.) In the project example that follows, the team will work each iteration for a period, then the project reviewers (SMEs, stakeholders, project sponsor, and learners) will have a week to review, cycling back and forth over the course of three iterations before final release.

**Figure 7-1.** Sample Top-Down Project Plan

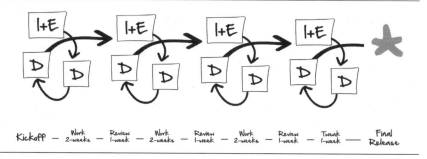

You can lay this out on a calendar or in a spreadsheet that looks something like this template for an e-learning project (Figure 7-2), showing the cycles of work and hand-off between the team and the SME and sponsor. We like to use this week-by-week layout to make it clear what happens on what weeks.

**Figure 7-2.** A Week-by-Week High-Level Project Schedule

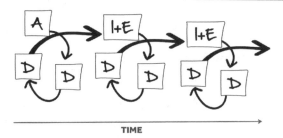

In this example, you might then look at this schedule and ask a few key questions (or review answers that may have been given earlier):

- When is the anticipated start date of the project?
- When does it need to be finished?
- When will the content and the SME be ready to work with us?
- When and how long will it take to review each iteration?
- Is this the right number of iterations?
- When are busy periods and slow periods for the SMEs? For reviewers?
- Are there any planned vacations or leaves of absence by key stakeholders or project team members?
- What other projects are the team members working on? What are the peak work periods for those projects?
- Will the project need legal or HR or other reviews? How long should we plan for that?

These questions become very relevant when you compare them to the actual work schedules of the people you need to work with you on the project—SMEs, reviewers, sponsors, and stakeholders. For example, you may find that SMEs may not have all the content ready for you to begin working immediately after the project kickoff session, or that a busy period in the business will fall right during a time when you need a review of the project deliverables. These high-level scheduling challenges will need to be worked out to arrive at a mutually agreed-upon delivery date for the project.

How do you solve high-level scheduling challenges? It depends on the nature of the challenge and the time availability and flexibility of the others you're working with. Some options include:

- moving the delivery date of the project
- relieving SMEs and reviewers of other work so they can prioritize this project's needs

- adding team members to the project
- reducing the scope of the project or only releasing parts of it in a phased approach
- identifying alternate SMEs or reviewers
- hiring outside resources to resolve capacity constraints.

In addition to the options above for dealing with scheduling challenges, here are some best practices for high-level scheduling:

- Avoid scheduling release dates for multiple projects all at once.
- Avoid scheduling many reviews for the same reviewers all at once.
- Allow for downtime or overruns between projects.
- Encourage team members and fellow project managers to participate in the high-level scheduling for the best allocation of resources and timelines.
- Remember that the project schedule is an estimate. The farther out it goes, the less likely it is to be completely accurate, so plan accordingly.
- Share the high-level schedule frequently with project stakeholders, SMEs, and reviewers.

# Bottom-Up Planning

The bottom-up project planning aligns tasks, team members, and resources with the top-down broad project schedule. If the goal for the current week is to deliver a high-level storyboard to the reviewers, then each of the tasks for the week must support that goal. The goal is for the team members to have at least as much time available to work on the project as the task estimates add up to. Of course, that's not always the case. If the task estimates are greater than the time available, you can choose to:

- Change the scope of the work to fit.
- Change the deadline.
- Add more team member resources.

Note that while you can plan for review periods, the work in between cannot be planned in detail because the team will not know what changes will come out of each review. The work periods after each review are merely high-level estimates, and you should resist the urge to predict those in great detail. This means that at the outset of the project, you make detailed plans to reach the first iteration review milestone, and make rough estimates for each review after that based on your best judgment and your experience with similar projects in the past (or guidance and suggestions from those who do).

In some cases, SMEs and others close to the project can provide guidance to the work estimates and the plan. You might consider sharing your project plan and asking for input. For example, your client might say either, "Oh, our material will be coming in from six different SMEs and will need to be reconciled—you should plan on that taking more than two weeks," or the opposite: "We've got this already pretty well pulled together in this other course that we do, so it shouldn't take you long to get through this."

As the project progresses, the bottom-up plan details will emerge as each iteration's changes come in and the team moves the deliverables forward.

## Putting the Two Plans Together

The top-down plan and the bottom-up plan are each useful components for the project. Where the two don't meet, there's an opportunity for discussion to resolve the impasse. Here's what it looks like for a project in which the sponsor's desired due date is after the date on which the team feels they can deliver (Figure 7-3). In this figure, think of the top-down plan as the high-level schedule for the project over time. The bottom-up schedule is the number of hours over that time period that need to be incurred to reach the project goals.

**Figure 7-3.** How Top-Down and Bottom-Up Plans Come Together:
When There's More Than Enough Time

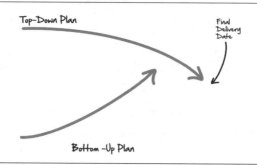

Most people will feel good about a project like this. Opportunities for discussion here include whether more should be added to the project, whether this team could take on more work or other projects at the same time, or if the sponsor wishes to release it earlier than planned.

Most instructional designers and project managers will tell you that their projects look more like the one in Figure 7-4, where the project sponsor wants the finished product sooner than the team feels it can be done. This is an opportunity to discuss whether reducing the scope, adding project resources, changing the delivery date, or taking other measures to meet the target will be necessary.

**Figure 7-4.** How Top-Down and Bottom-Up Plans Come Together:
When There's More Work to Do Than a Project Delivery Date Allows

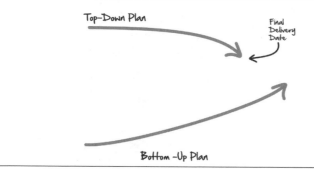

In most projects, the bottom-up plan is not a nice smooth line of work effort progressing cumulatively over time. With alternating intense periods of work and less intense times when the deliverables are being reviewed, you might find a project typically progresses more like the one in Figure 7-5. The bottom-up plan shows hours increasing in spurts of development, then leveling off while the deliverables are being reviewed and the team is not actively working on this project.

**Figure 7-5.** Work Done in Spurts With Periods of Review

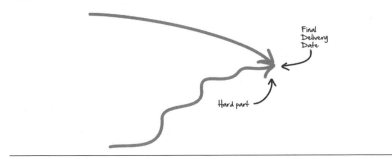

## Plan for the Unexpected

It might seem as though having the two plans reach the same point on the same date would be most desirable, like the one in Figure 7-5, where the project team's detailed bottom-up plan shows they will finish the project right on the due date desired by the project sponsor. While this seems like an ideal situation, you should expect changes to pop up as new needs are identified. Changes to the project along the way in a project plan like the one in Figure 7-5, where there's no space to accommodate them, are risky.

As a result, each project should have a contingency for both time and resources to accommodate the inevitable bumps on the road (Figure 7-6).

**Figure 7-6.** Estimates for Project Include Time Contingency Before the Due Date

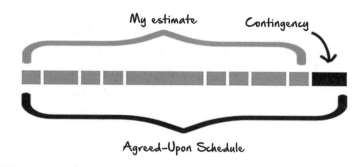

The size of this contingency is based on the project's overall risk. The contingency you add would typically be between 5 percent and 15 percent of the project's total hours or days, but you will determine this based on your experience and comfort level. Factors that affect risk—and increase your need for contingency time—typically include:

- technical difficulty
- content difficulty
- stability of the subject/content
- whether it's a first-time project with this sponsor or SME
- experience with this project sponsor or type of project
- sometimes, the project sponsor's insight into the project's risk.

Chapter 2 included a sidebar on how to assess these and other risks.

## Tools for Visual Planning

Agile teams plan visually, which can make the project status incredibly easy to identify at any moment. Traditionally these plans are in physical format—sticky notes, corkboards, and so on. Online project management tools can be used to support virtual teams, although these tools have the disadvantage of a limited screen size across which to display large projects or many multiple components at once.

In our team's office, we used to use a series of six large corkboards like a big analog spreadsheet to display all our high-level project arcs in a central area. Here are two of the pieces of what we affectionately call "the big board" (Figure 7-7).

**Figure 7-7.** TorranceLearning's Big Board

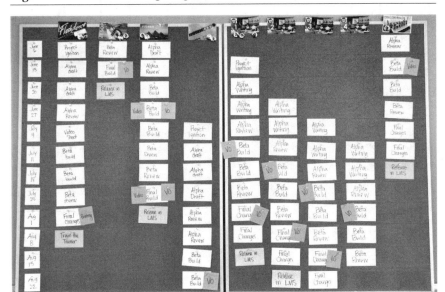

On this board, each row is a week, and each column is a different project. We use code names on our projects because these boards are out in the open for passersby to see. The project team's work is summarized for each week using 3x5 index cards.

Take a look at the first project (Project Flashdance) in Figure 7-8. This project kicks off the week of June 6. That ignition included some rough prototyping, followed by two weeks of work for a first draft (alpha). The week of June 27 is a review week—the team rests (or does other work) while the client team and representative learners review and use the deliverables and provide feedback. Then the team picks up for three weeks of video shooting and development work. A one-week review of the next iteration (beta) is scheduled for the week of July 25, to be followed by an estimated single week of final tweaks and printing before a train-the-trainer is scheduled for the week of August 8.

On this board, we color code the index cards as follows so it's easy to scan across and see who is doing what and when:

- White cards are the work to be done by the project team.
- Yellow cards signify review weeks.
- Green cards are release or hand-over weeks.
- Purple cards indicate needed resources from outside our own project team.

For larger projects with multiple components, we tend to stagger the start dates of each component. This allows us to smooth out the work for the team, spread out the load on the reviewers, and apply what we've learned through earlier segments to later ones. Figure 7-9 is an example of a staggered start project with four "swim lanes," or workstreams.

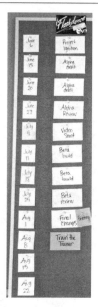

**Figure 7-8.** Project Flashdance

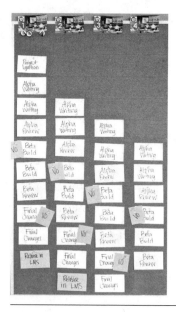

**Figure 7-9.** Staggered Start Dates

Note in the project above that the review team only sees one component in each week, except for one week in which they have both the first and the fourth swim lanes' deliverables to review. This is an e-learning course and we have similarly spread out the work effort for the voice-over artist (the purple VO cards). In this case, both reviewers and outside partners can schedule their time accordingly.

Of course, at the intersection of the weeks for any of these projects on the big board are a number of tasks that the team needs to carry out to reach each iterative milestone. This is the bottom-up detailed plan where the team focuses most of their attention.

To do this in a traditional, analog fashion, we lay out our weekly tasks on a corkboard for each project, with swim lanes for the team members and rows for the days of the week (Figure 7-10).

**Figure 7-10.** Weekly Project Board for an E-Learning Project With Swim Lanes

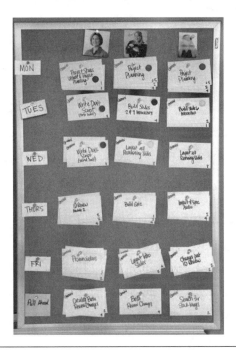

Each team member sets out his or her tasks on the week's schedule based on the time estimates for each one, carefully accounting for standing meetings, days off work, and other job responsibilities as tasks are allocated. If there are tasks to be completed that don't fit within the week's schedule, they're put in a "pull ahead" row at the bottom of the corkboard, so that if work is completed faster than estimated, everyone knows what should be worked on next.

As the work is completed, its status is updated so that a visual and real-time status update can be obtained at any time. Agile tasks are typically color coded to denote status. With the LLAMA approach, we use the following colors:

- No color—the task has not been started.
- Yellow—the task is in progress.
- Green—the task is completed.
- Blue—we are waiting on something before this can be completed.
- Red—something has gone wrong with this task.

These detailed weekly project plans are updated each week based on the work completed in the prior week and input from the project sponsor regarding priorities and changes. With an Agile project management approach, it becomes easy for team members to track their hours spent on a project at a task-by-task level since they are doing this anyway with the work estimates. This supports allocations within organizations or direct billing by vendors on an hourly basis.

The corkboard approach with personal swim lanes works well for smaller, straightforward projects without a lot of moving parts when the team is co-located and the board can be easily displayed for all to see. Since that might not apply to your organization (it no longer applies to TorranceLearning in 2019), you can adopt an online approach with a different layout that accommodates larger teams using the free project management tools like Trello. Other tools accommodate a similar approach. Here's a sample project board in Trello (Figure 7-11).

**Figure 7-11.** Trello Board of Weekly Tasks

The layout for this board is inspired by kanban. Kanban is a Japanese manufacturing and inventory approach that roughly translates to "card" or "visual sign." In a kanban system, the flow of work is visualized through the process, and the number of simultaneous pieces of work in progress are limited. On this board, each task is a card and work flows from left to right through each of the lists.

- **Backlog**—The backlog is the list of all the known work that must be done. For tasks related to future iterations, you can write at a very high level as you might not yet know the details that you will receive from the iteration reviews. While you don't have to put every task that is envisioned out for many months in advance, this is a handy place to put future work items you know you'll need to remember. In many cases the items listed in the backlog are not defined well enough to actually work on yet.

- **Defined and Ready**—Once an item from the backlog has enough detail that it can be worked on, that detail is documented on the card and it moves to this list. Agile software development teams call the process of this definition "grooming."

- **Weekly Backlog**—These tasks are ones that will be accomplished in this week or this iteration. The team has determined there is sufficient time to work on these tasks.

- **WIP**—When a team member picks up a card and starts working on it, it moves into this column. The goal is to limit the number of items in this column, to avoid multitasking and switch-tasking, which can be inefficient. One of the goals of Agile is to maximize throughput of work, and one of the most important ways we do this is by minimizing the number of items that are started but not yet finished. Typically a card is only assigned to a person when it reaches this column, although it may have been assigned back in the weekly backlog, particularly if there are skill specialties that make assigning a particular card to a particular person meaningful.

- **QA**—This column indicates work that is ready to be reviewed by another teammate or out for the review team to look at.

- **Done**—Once the task is ready to be delivered, you can place it in this column.

Most Agile software products (and Trello is no exception) allow for you to write additional notes in detail within each card to keep track of specific sub-tasks related to that card. This becomes a very helpful place to write the detail that is needed to communicate from one team member to another about how best to complete a task or the particular pieces of it.

Whether you choose to use index cards on a corkboard or online tools, the goal of a visual management system is to make it clear to everybody at any point in the project exactly what the status of the work is.

## What Could Possibly Go Wrong?

Common issues with project planning include:

**You don't take the time to plan.** It is not unusual for L&D teams to be asked to just skip the planning process (and all the time that it takes) for projects that are very small or are so tight on resources that the client does not care to "waste" those resources on planning. Those are exactly the projects that need the most planning!

**Team members fail to update task status.** What makes a visual system like this work is the task updates made by each team member as they do their work.

**You are overwhelmed by (or overconfident in) your ability to plan all the future tasks for a project.** Unless you can predict the future, you will waste a fair amount of time and effort trying to predict every future task that you will need to do on a project. It is typically sufficient to estimate one to two weeks at a time, referencing back to the high-level arc of the project.

## Key Takeaways

- Plan both the high-level arc of a project and the bottom-up estimate so that you can determine whether you have enough time and resources to reach the desired end point on the desired end date.
- Plan your work visually and update work items frequently so the project's status is always apparent.
- Choose a digital or analog tool to help you in this process.

# CHAPTER 8

# Define and Estimate Tasks

**In This Chapter**
- What are the challenges in making estimates?
- What are the four rules for estimating tasks?
- How do you respond when an estimate is wrong?

A longtime client of ours once had a strange request—an interesting challenge we wanted to help him out with, even though it had nothing to do with learning per se. He had been using a piece of software to accomplish a decision-making and lightly computational task, and he was about to lose access to this software. He asked if we could rebuild the software in Articulate Storyline because, while he wasn't a programmer, he did know Storyline. By building the program in Storyline, he'd be able to manage and make updates himself in the future.

So how much would it cost?

We had no idea whatsoever.

But, we had a process for estimating, so Matt Kliewer (our lead
Storyline mastermind at the time) and
I sat down and got to work. The client
laid out for us the 72 possible steps the
software would take, each on a differ-
ent screen, to accomplish its task. We sorted those screens into four groups:

- text-only informational screens
- simple data entry screens that stored a variable but didn't
  calculate anything
- screens that made a simple calculation or rule-based
  determination that we (well, Matt) knew how to build
- screens that we had no idea how to build (fortunately there were
  only three of these).

We then estimated how long it would take to build each type, using one
of the Agile techniques for estimating that you'll learn in this chapter:

- text-only informational screens = four per hour
- simple data entry screens that stored a variable, but didn't
  calculate anything = one hour each
- screens that made a simple calculation or rule-based
  determination that we knew how to build = two hours each
- screens that we had no idea how to build = eight hours each.

Matt would be doing the work, so he created the estimates. We then
counted the screens in each category and in under an hour—and with no
gnashing of teeth—we'd determined an estimate for the project.

With the project officially kicked off, you understand the learner personas, you have scoped out the project, and you have agreed to the project's

parameters. You finally have all the information you need to get started. Now, it's time to get down to work. Right? Not so fast.

The worst thing you could do right now is start working on the project!

Without a plan and an estimate for completing the tasks it will take to get here, you will not know whether you can meet your deadline in any sort of reasonable fashion. Reaching that deadline requires a delicate dance between the high-level timeline of activities (what I called the "arc of the project plan" in chapter 7) and the detailed estimate of tasks you'll complete along the way. Where the top-down arc to the project deadline and the bottom-up estimate of the tasks don't meet, that's when you start having conversations with the project sponsor about what to do next.

## The Challenges of Estimating

"How long does it take to create a course?" If you've been in this profession any length of time, you've been asked this question at some point by a well-meaning project sponsor. It's not an unreasonable question at all. And, of course, you can point to research by Bryan Chapman and the Chapman Alliance in 2010 and by Robyn Defelice and Karl Kapp in 2017 that provides guidelines about what it takes to develop an hour of training material. Yet most of us have pretty sheepish answers to this question, in part because we usually don't have a lot of information yet when this question is asked and in part because "a course" is so big that it's often hard to tell. Few of us will want to be held to the Chapman or Defelice and Kapp numbers in reality.

The concept of "a course" has a lot of range to it, so let's work with something a bit more concrete. Here's an activity you can do to teach some of the underlying concepts and fallacies in estimating. It works best in a group of five or more people, and all you'll need is some clear glassware of varying sizes and a bunch of candy (feel free to eat it afterward). Start with a big container like a water pitcher. Ask the group to estimate how many jelly beans are in the pitcher (Figure 8-1), and write down the answers.

**Figure 8-1.** A Large Container of Jelly Beans—Hard to Estimate

Calculate an average of all the answers. Sometimes it's close to the actual number of jelly beans. And sometimes it's laughably off. Calculate the range in the answers—the difference between the highest estimate and the lowest estimate. The range is usually huge. Even the groups that manage to get an average guess that's close to the actual number of jelly beans are quite humbled by the range of the answers they provided. It's clear that they've only accidentally stumbled upon an accurate figure.

Then fill a smaller container, like a glass, with jelly beans, and ask them to estimate the number (Figure 8-2).

**Figure 8-2.** A Medium Sized Container of Jelly Beans—Easier to Estimate

Again, calculate the average, calculate the range, and have someone actually count the jelly beans. What the group will learn here is that their average estimate is usually closer to the actual, that the range of answers is tighter (in proportion to the number of jelly beans), and that it takes a long time to count how many jelly beans are in this glass. (And everyone's really glad I didn't ask them to count the ones in the big pitcher a few minutes ago!)

And finally, while everyone's busy munching on candies, bring out an even smaller glass (Figure 8-3). Repeat the estimating and your calculations.

**Figure 8-3.** A Very Small Container of Jelly Beans—Easiest to Estimate

All of a sudden the group is really good at this. Their average is pretty close to the actual number of jelly beans, and the range is pretty tight. Every time. And it takes less than a minute to count the jelly beans to verify whether our estimate was close or not.

What does this tell us about estimating? Humans are really bad at it, and we do better with small quantities.

## Estimating Work Effort, Not Duration or Deadline

Keep in mind that when estimating, you are estimating the work effort to complete a task and not the duration of time before it can be delivered. Here's an easy way to understand the distinction. Let's say that first thing on Monday morning you hire a lawyer who bills by the hour to spend an hour reviewing a contract. She can start work on this at 4 p.m. on Friday and deliver her comments to you by 5 p.m. on Friday. You would expect to pay for the lawyer's effort—one hour—not the duration of time since you received your contract back—40 hours.

Obviously the work effort and the delivery date are related. We need to know the amount of work that will be required before we can commit to a delivery date. And the delivery date may inform how much effort we can spend on the work. But the two are distinct concepts, and we get ourselves into trouble if we conflate them.

## How Long Will It Take?

Of course, your manager or the project sponsor doesn't want you to demonstrate the challenge of estimating big tasks by counting jelly beans. They will still want to know, "How long does it take to create a course?" To answer, you might benefit from turning that hard question into an easier one. "How long does it take to write a paragraph?" Or, "to create one quiz question?" Or, "to build a three-screen scenario?"

Now, those questions have somewhat more concrete answers. Not perfect, but you're probably more sure of them. Why? Because, just like the small glass of jelly beans, the smaller size of the effort makes it easier to estimate. That's the first rule of estimating. Let's cover that and three other rules in more detail.

### In LLAMA, We Estimate by Task

Agile software teams estimate functional user stories. In instructional design, I recommend you estimate tasks. Software teams are typically dedicated to a single project and each team member can fully develop each story. Instructional designers are typically juggling many projects at once, and our work may involve several hand-offs. As such, it is far more useful to estimate and plan at the small-task level.

Consider estimating in tasks that are no larger than half a day. For very skilled team members or very nebulous tasks, you might go up to tasks of a whole day. This is highly unusual, though.

# Rule #1: Break Things Into the Smallest Feasible Chunks

While an Agile software team will often estimate their work effort by the story, instructional designers rarely have the luxury of focusing on a single project at a time. Thus, try to break down each piece of the project into subtasks and estimate at that level. This allows you to work on a task for one project, complete it, and then switch to a task from another project (if we must). And, because of the smaller size, you have a better shot at having an estimate that's close to the reality of what it will take.

When breaking the work down into tasks, aim for the following:

- **Each task is discrete.** Reviewing a piece of content with a subject matter expert and making updates to the topic as a result of that review are two separate tasks that need to be estimated and planned as such.
- **Each task is completed by a single person.** In theory, if a meeting will involve several people, it can be written as a single task for each person. In practice, this is a bit cumbersome. This concept is helpful for planning and estimating, though, because a single one-hour meeting with six people actually consumes six hours of available working time.
- **Each task takes between 30 minutes and four hours of contiguous time to complete.** If it will take more than four hours, break it down into smaller sub-tasks. If it will take less than half an hour, put it on a to-do list. Then carve out time each day to accomplish the to-do list items.
- **Each task can be completed.** That might sound silly, but it's important that each task actually be something you or a team member can complete. "Make it prettier" is not a completable task because there's too much judgment involved and it could

be a never-ending process. "Update graphic elements to the new style guide" is a more completable task.

# Rule #2: The Person Who Does the Work Estimates the Work

Larger Agile teams will estimate their stories as a team. Each person gives an estimate for each story, and the mode (the figure that appears the most often) is used as the team's estimate for high-level planning purposes. However, when it comes time to actually do the work, the individual's own estimate is the one that prevails. That works for large software teams made up of generalists.

On smaller teams (like with most instructional design projects), there usually aren't enough people to participate in a group estimating activity, so the individual assigned to a particular task is the one to estimate it. This is a key point here: The project manager is not the one estimating the work effort. While the project manager may communicate the value of the task and the amount of time available for it, the individual is the one to estimate the work effort. Where the individual's estimate and the project manager's allotted time don't match up, that's a signal that a conversation is needed.

In practice, I have found two exceptions to this rule:

1. If you've never done a task, it's OK to ask someone what their estimate would be.
2. If a task is nebulous in scope, the project sponsor (or project manager) should provide a timebox around it based on its value to the overall project. For example, if a particular topic's content included "research the best practices for mentoring new supervisors in a peanut butter processing environment," that could be accomplished with a web search in 0.3 seconds . . . or a doctoral student could conduct some primary research

and write a dissertation on the topic in three years. In this case, the value to the project sponsor is what drives the work effort allotted to it, and this generally requires some conversation and negotiation.

# Rule #3: Don't Pad Your Estimate

This rule is the single most difficult one to get used to, in my experience, because most of us have worked in situations in which something bad happens if we are not able to deliver on time. Fear is a powerful motivator. To prevent these negative consequences, or simply in an effort to under-promise and over-deliver, many people fall into the trap of adding some extra padding to an estimate "just to be safe." This is a completely natural and understandable response, and it's one that perpetuates a culture based on fear and lies.

There's an old *Dilbert* cartoon in which Dilbert is asked by his pointy-haired boss for an estimate to fix a bug in some software. A thought bubble above his head shows "two hours" and the speech bubble says "two days." Moving to the next panel, the pointy-haired boss is asked by his boss how long it will take Dilbert to fix the bug, and he replies, "two weeks." On the next panel, the estimate has become "two months." It arrives on the CEO's desk as, "It will take Dilbert two years to fix this. Do you want to do it?"

Of course, the CEO can choose to say yes or no. If the answer is "no" then everyone is happy—there is less work to do. But if the answer is "yes," even in Dilbert's world no one is so completely incompetent that this bug can't be fixed in two years' time.

However, everyone—except Dilbert—is operating based on false information. When every task has a padding factor, we lose track of what the actual work effort will be.

# Rule #4: Account for the Uncertainty of Large Things

Some tasks are just larger than other tasks and don't really have any good means of being broken down into smaller pieces. That means that your estimate for these larger tasks is likely to be farther afield than the estimates for your smaller tasks. The technique underlying the fourth rule of estimating takes this into account.

Take a look at these two sequences—they have something in common:

### Powers of Two

1.2.4.8.16.32.64

### Fibonacci Sequence

1.2.3.5.8.13.21.34.55

As the sequence progresses, the difference between any two adjacent numbers is greater. That is, as things get bigger, they get less granular. And that's exactly how to handle the uncertainty of large things in Agile.

The team decides on which sequence to use and always selects a number from that sequence when we estimate. This forces a discipline that enables us to make rapid and sufficiently accurate estimates. When we're estimating tasks, the unit we estimate in is hours. When we estimate larger pieces of work, particularly at the outset of a project when we're determining the overall planning arc, we may estimate in days, weeks, or even months.

This can be an uncomfortable approach to get used to. Here are the common questions you or your project teammates might be asking about estimating this way.

## Which Sequence Should Our Team Use?

When my team and I first started using Agile, we learned from a mentor, Rich Sheridan, who used the powers of two. In fact, Rich and his teams at

Menlo Innovations call their estimating method Planning Origami. Their planning and estimating is done on paper, and the task estimating lets them plan a week of work very visually. A week's worth of work—32 hours—is represented on a full sheet of paper. Fold it in half for a 16-hour piece of work. Fold it in half again for an eight-hour piece. And so on, for four, two, and the difficult to fold one-hour unit of work. They can then assemble tasks to fill a 32-hour week and tape everything together.

Our teams used the powers of two estimating (although not the Origami Planning) for several years until we discovered the Scrum for Trello Chrome extension. This extension has a card-estimating function that uses the Fibonacci Sequence, so, for no other reason than the switch to a tool that would do the calculations for us, we switched and have been using Fibonacci ever since. The added benefit of the Fibonacci sequence is that there is a lot of convenient granularity around the smaller tasks that we tend to work with in instructional design.

## What If I Believe a Task Should Take Six Hours?

Regardless of the sequence you use, **six** is not an available option. There are two ways to handle this situation.

One way is to break down the task to two three-hour tasks, or three two-hour tasks. This approach has the added benefit providing a built-in opportunity to confirm or adjust your estimate for the remaining work after you reach each of the internal milestones.

The other way is the "bucket approach." It goes like this: If you have six gallons of water to carry, would you use an eight-gallon bucket or a five-gallon bucket? Most people choose the eight-gallon bucket. That's your estimate.

## Isn't Padding Being Built Into These Sequences?

There's a fine distinction between accounting for uncertainty and intentionally padding for protection. It's all about mindset, really.

Whether you're using Agile methods or not, your estimates are just that: estimates. You are human. Humans are generally bad at estimating.

Tom Root, a managing partner at Zingerman's Mailorder at the time and one of the most structured thinkers I know, once told me, "The only thing we know about a forecast is that it's wrong." (Of course, he's not the first person so say this.) The same goes for estimating. An estimate is just an estimate. It's not a quote or a budget, and it's definitely not a promise. In some cases it's a target, but a good Agile estimate should be a realistic target, not an aspirational one.

This is an important message, though, for you, your teammates, the people you work for, and the people who work for you. It may represent a significant cultural shift to fully embrace this aspect of Agile. That said, it's important to be careful with your clients to explain what you mean by estimates. Deadlines are when you deliver. They may be hard and immovable. But the work effort that you will undergo to get there will be measured in estimates.

## When the Estimate Is Wrong

If an estimate is just an estimate, what do you do when it turns out be wrong? This is an opportunity for communication and learning. There are five steps to take when an estimate is wrong.

### Five Steps for When the Estimate Is Wrong
1. Speak up as soon as you know.
2. Say "Thank you!"
3. Understand why.
4. Figure out what to do next.
5. Tell whomever you need to about it.

1. **Speak up as soon as you know.** As soon as it's evident that an estimate is materially inaccurate (as defined by your team and your scheduling tolerances), it's time to speak up. If you've worked

five hours on a three-hour task, you're at least two hours overdue in raising a flag. The trust and accountability inherent in an Agile project demands you let your teammates know when something has gone awry.

2. **Say "Thank you!"** While you may not like the message, you are now more informed than you were 10 minutes ago. If you yell at the person who just told you their estimate was wrong, you'll soon find that you don't hear about wrong estimates as much anymore. It's not that the estimates will get much better—you just won't know about it anymore. This breeds fear and results in disinformation.

3. **Understand why.** You need to understand why the estimate was off. Did you not have enough information beforehand? Did you poorly understand the scope? Use an inefficient approach? Wildly efficient approach? Completely missed a big chunk of the need? In order to take the next steps, it's important to understand why we're here.

4. **Figure out what to next.** Based on the scale of the missed estimation and the reasons why, determine a course of action to get back on schedule.

5. **Tell whomever about it you need to.** In most cases, a single-task under- or over-estimation is not worthy of discussion with the project sponsor. Your goal as the project manager, however, is to keep an eye on the general trend of things and determine when to communicate. Usually, the earlier you communicate, the better.

When the project as a whole is running over the estimates, you can problem solve with the project team and the project sponsor. Should you reduce scope? Is the overage OK because the project is worthy of it? Should the team find ways to be more efficient? Can outside developers or additional stakeholders and SMEs be brought in to help?

When the project is running under your original estimates, that's often a happier conversation. Can you now accomplish some things that were originally considered out of scope? Have you missed something important and that's why you're under the estimate? Do you get to finish early and start a next phase or start something new?

All of these options—and more—can be discussed with the project sponsor more clearly because you have data at a detailed level that helps you see into the projected end of the project.

## What Could Possibly Go Wrong?

Common issues with estimating include:

**You pad the estimates.** Resist the urge to add a little to a task estimate "just to be safe." Those bits of padding to every task on a project add up and, over time, inflate the project. While we feel like stars for under-promising and over-delivering, the truth is that that heroic delivery started with a lie. Over time, this is a dysfunctional behavior in an organization.

**You estimate too far in advance.** Every day you learn something more about the project you're working on—and quite often that affects the tasks you work on and their estimates. Successful Agile teams estimate no further out than one to two weeks so each estimate is based on the most current information.

**You think about estimating duration instead of effort.** The estimate of the work effort required to complete a task is related to the date on which you can deliver it, but they are distinct concepts. It's entirely possible that a task only takes one hour, but you will do it next week. Both of these pieces of information (effort estimate and delivery date) are useful but should not be conflated.

**You create a false sense of precision.** Elaborate schedules and estimates with specific numbers (even decimals!) give the appearance of precision, while offering no additional accuracy because it is all an estimate. In fact, the more precise the numbers appear to be, the more you risk communicating that these are the numbers, where a rounded number or a range conveys that this is just an estimate (Figure 8-4).

**Figure 8-4.** Ranges of Estimation Precision

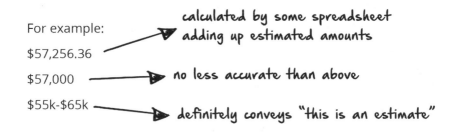

## Key Takeaways

- Without a plan and an estimate for completing the tasks it will take to get here, you will not know whether you can meet your deadline.
- Humans are really bad at estimating. Don't over-rely on your ability to estimate accurately.
- Follow the rules for estimating:
  - » Rule #1: Break things into the smallest feasible chunks.
  - » Rule #2: The person who does the work estimates the work.
  - » Rule #3: Estimate based on what you think it will take to do the work, with no padding.
  - » Rule #4: Account for the uncertainty of large things.
- An estimate is just that—an estimate.

# CHAPTER 9

# Design and Deliver in Iterations

**In This Chapter**
- Why should you break a project into iterations?
- What is a minimum viable product?
- How do you iterate and gather feedback before project completion?

Several years ago, my team and I were engaged to develop a mentoring program for a manufacturer of automotive and industrial components on what we code named Project Buddy. Engineers were the lifeblood of this innovative and successful company and the labor market for talented engineers was tight. HR identified a retention problem: Many young engineers would leave the company just after their one-year anniversary; but those that did not leave would often stay on for a decade or more. Their goal was to create a mentoring program to enhance the connection with the company in an effort to retain a greater percentage of new hires after that critical first-year mark. This mentoring program would be focused on social connections, and HR was concerned that the engineer mentors would not have the interpersonal skills required for the task. Part of our training effort to accompany the program was to help experienced engineers form appropriate social bonds without being too awkwardly personal.

There's a lot of nuance involved in something like this, and I was of the opinion that we didn't need to be too specific in the e-learning course. I thought, these are adults holding down jobs, with families and friends and community connections. They had not been fired or reprimanded at work for inappropriate behavior. Surely we didn't need to define in-bounds and out-of-bounds questions for the "getting to know you" part of the mentoring relationship. The HR team disagreed.

Our solution was to build a face-to-face, instructor-led course to gauge the level at which we needed to provide instruction on this topic. While the content was the same, the delivery and the activities were tailored to a face-to-face environment. Meg Fairchild, the lead instructional designer on the project, and I could co-teach the session and see what the reaction was firsthand. As we got to the part of the class where we were outlining the first meeting between the mentor and the mentee, we watched carefully. Were they offended? Annoyed? Bored? No! They were taking notes. Turned out I was wrong!

Egos firmly intact, we had the opportunity to learn this crucial thing about the learners and the course we were building while it was still a relatively inexpensive face-to-face class, before we built everything in a more costly e-learning format. Is it more time- and resource-intensive to build ILT before building e-learning? Of course! But it's a lot less expensive than building out the wrong e-learning course, which we would have done if I had my way.

What's more, after the pilot ILT class, we polished a few things and gave it to the client HR team to run while we proceeded with the e-learning build. Whenever they had a group of mentors-to-be, they could run the in-person class. I got a call a few weeks later from a surprised and satisfied HR team member who was thrilled to be receiving value from the work that we were doing together before the project was even finished.

## Iterations and Instructional Design

One of the defining features of Agile project management—the one most visible to project sponsors and stakeholders—is iterative development. This is the primary mechanism by which the team, the SMEs, the sponsor, and project stakeholders are continually learning more about the project as it progresses. Agile is inherently a learning process (even for teams who are not creating a learning product).

Most project teams will already find themselves creating successive drafts of a product before release. In this respect, iterative development is not really news. However, most teams are not getting the full benefit of each iteration, and the shift here could be as much a cultural shift in how a team works within the organization as it is a project procedural change.

With LLAMA, you release a workable product earlier in the development process than with a traditional waterfall-shaped ADDIE approach to a project. Agile is both iterative and incremental. Each release can be both an iterative improvement upon what was last released and incrementally larger in scope or more built-out. The goal is to learn as much as possible about what works before progressing on a project. Compare representations of the two project management approaches in Figure 9-1.

**Figure 9-1.** ADDIE and LLAMA

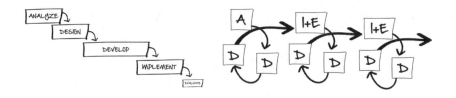

You could think of it like editions of a textbook, in which the first edition is useful, but the second edition often includes richer descriptions, factual updates, and clarifications around things that readers of the first edition found confusing. Over time, the author might release field guides or workshops based on the book that address deeper needs that some smaller audiences may find useful, although these generally have a smaller readership than the full book. Over the years, by time the 17th edition of the book is released, there are few—if any—significant changes introduced. At this point, individual facts are being updated and case studies are refreshed, and it may very well be that the 15th, 16th, and 17th editions are essentially interchangeable.

## Why Iterate?

If the concept of iterating is really similar to draft reviews that many teams do, what's the big deal? The key to an Agile iteration is in the who and why of the reviews. Where many instructional design teams will get mid-progress reviews from SMEs and project stakeholders, they are often not getting the product in front of actual learners and thus missing an opportunity to see if the product really works with *people who don't already know the content*. That's not to say that SMEs and sponsors don't have an important role to play—they're critical!—but if you fail to include the learners, you lose out on a valuable set of data.

An iterative approach is also designed to help you identify mistakes early when they are usually less costly to fix and overall keep the project on track with what the learners need. There are several side benefits of the iterative process that shouldn't go unmentioned.

First, you always have a running version of the program. Should budgets get cut, priorities change, or you get too busy to get back to it (these things never happen in corporate education—wink!), the current workable iteration could serve sufficiently to train people. You have something to show for your efforts, and the organization has a workable product that can be used, albeit without all the bells and whistles that could have been put on it.

Second, since you're only identifying tasks and estimating work one iteration at a time, the whole process is much simpler and less speculative. The team works with much more reasonable estimates based on information gathered recently rather than guesses made at the project kickoff that may have happened months ago.

And third, it's just psychologically more satisfying to celebrate small releases as each iteration is completed and put out for review. This is an opportunity for you as the project lead to take care of yourself and the team with a congratulatory pause, if not a full-on celebration of the accomplishment.

## Megan's Rules for Iterations
- It does real work.
- Someone else has to use it.
- You gather data.
- Data informs the work to do in the next iteration.

## How Iterative Design Works

Here's how iterative design works: On a regular basis, the team releases a version of the product that is a minimum viable product—the MVP—for review, partial release, or even full release. The goal is to gather insights about whether:

- The product meets the project parameters.
- The content is accurate and sufficiently complete.
- The learners can use it to learn and better accomplish the performance objective.
- The original question is still valid. (Are we solving the right problem? In the right way?)

## What's the Difference Between an MVP and a Prototype?

A prototype is a useful tool in the idea generation phase. Teams will often develop several prototypes and use them to try out a variety of concepts in the early days and weeks of a project. Prototypes are generally not workable versions that can be used by learners or customers. Most digital prototypes will be set aside when development work begins as they may not have been created in the tools that will be used for the finished product.

An MVP, in contrast, is an actual working product, version, or course that can be used with learners. It is considerably further along in development than a prototype and it will evolve over time. MVPs may take weeks or months to create.

An Agile software team will typically work in a "sprint" period of one to two weeks, then release a product iteration every sprint or every several sprints. (Think of your favorite web-based software. Does it feel like it updates every week? Exactly!) I've found that Agile instructional design teams typically work from one to three weeks per iteration and can release an iteration for review every cycle. While the flow of work for most software teams is continuous (each sprint starts the day after the previous one ends), most instructional design teams will pause their development work while waiting for feedback.

Let's run through two examples of what an iterative project workflow might look like as part of the project planning cycles discussed in chapter 7. First is a team developing traditional e-learning:

Week 1: Write course outline and flow

Week 2: Course outline is reviewed by SME and client team
▶ FIRST ITERATION

Week 3: Write course storyboard and script

Week 4: Write course storyboard and script

Week 5: Review storyboard and script ▶ SECOND ITERATION

Week 6: Build working course draft

Week 7: Build working course draft

Week 8: Review working course draft ▶ THIRD ITERATION

Week 9: Finalize course

Week 10: Finalize course

Week 11: Release course ▶ FOURTH ITERATION

Second is a team developing traditional facilitated training:

Week 1: Write course outline and flow

Week 2: Course outline is reviewed by SME and client team
▶ FIRST ITERATION

Week 3: Write facilitator guide and slide decks

Week 4: Write facilitator guide and slide decks

Week 5: Review facilitator guide and slide decks
▶ SECOND ITERATION

Week 6: Write participant guide and activities

Week 7: Write participant guide and activities

Week 8: Conduct pilot class ▶ THIRD ITERATION

Week 9: Finalize course

Week 10: Finalize course

Week 11: Release course with full class session
▶ FOURTH ITERATION

Contrast these two examples with the ADDIE approach. In either case, you wouldn't have delivered a product to be tested until week 11. But now, with either the e-learning module or the in-person facilitated training, you've had opportunities to analyze the MVP along the way (weeks two, five, and eight), allowing for possible changes in wording or other elements.

Note that in the two above examples, you have three mid-project iterations with a fourth at the end. It may be difficult to get members of the actual learner population involved in testing each iteration. Sometimes they're customers that you might feel shy about bothering or they're workers who are very busy. It might just be politically inconvenient within the organization to draw learners away from their regular jobs. In that case, you can include proxies for the actual learners (and let them know that that's the lens through which you'd like their input). In addition to the learner proxies that you can ask to participate in the project kickoff, others include salespeople or business analysts who gather needs from the target audience or people who fit in the target audience but perhaps have already been trained in some way.

So, a typical iteration review may include input from the following people:

- members of the primary learner audience or their proxies—to determine whether the training actually works
- SME—for content accuracy
- project sponsor—for message alignment and strategic direction
- stakeholders—for overall project buy-in and their portion of content accuracy
- fellow instructional designers—for instructional soundness and adherence to quality standards
- system testers/QA (digital projects)—for interaction and data accuracy (this group may include formal software testing, LMS administrators to test for completion tracking)

- editors—for proofreading and adherence to quality standards
- legal, compliance, audit, HR—for adherence to their unique requirements.

That's a lot of reviewers! It's entirely reasonable to not have every one on every review cycle. Review roles are something that you will typically lay out early in the project so you can get on the right calendars and get the right people assembled (see chapter 2).

Note: Smaller projects will have shorter timeframes. Larger projects will not have larger timeframes, but rather break the large deliverable into several smaller ones with staggered starts. Some projects will have shorter or longer review periods. See the discussion in chapter 7.

Regardless of the timing or size of the project, at each review cycle a new round of design and development begins. New tasks are created, estimated, and assigned for development with a target to release the next iteration of the workable product in a short timeframe.

## Ways to Iterate

Defining iterative cycles is usually not difficult, and you may already be doing some form of review process already. Here are a few ideas:

**Alpha > Beta > Final**—This is described in the samples above, where "alpha" is a rough and simple version, "beta" is a more workable product, and the "final" or "gold" version is the one released to learners. Some projects will have more iterations, but few have fewer than these.

**By Module or Topic**—Breaking large projects down into each module or topic will allow for learning that occurs in the review cycles of earlier modules to influence the development of future modules. Using this approach, you typically start working with the content that is most ready, with the SMEs who are most available to work. This allows the team to get moving quickly and spend less time waiting even if you're not working in numerical order.

## You Don't Have to Start With the First Module

Consider this example: My team and I worked on a module-by-module basis on a project. Project Step was funded for one module of what was envisioned to be a six-module course on spinal cord injury assessment. The first module was to be shown to potential funding partners to solicit donations for the remaining five modules. This meant that we had one opportunity to make a splash.

Knowing the general feel of the six modules, here's what we had to choose from:

- Module 1 was to be a relatively mundane overview of anatomy and physiology; its content was stable, but it would require a lot of medical illustration.
- Modules 2-4 each covered a section of the examination of a patient's spinal cord function. Modules 2 and 3 would require significant illustration and a lot of committee input to get the nuance of the content correct. The project sponsor happened to be the lead SME for module 4, and he already had much of his thinking in order. What's more, because of the nature of the module, it would have fewer medical illustrations than the others so it would be faster and less costly.
- Module 5 pulled all the exam data together to create a score for the patient. The SME in charge of this module was incredibly busy, plus the content for it was still under committee discussion.
- Module 6 would be the additional optional testing. Its content would evolve as the project progressed and would make for a poor sample module for funding anyway.

Looking at it this way, it became pretty clear that module 4 should be the first one for development, and that's what we chose. That module was completed at low cost, quickly, and used successfully to secure funding for the rest of the program. If we had started with module 1, not only would it have taken longer to design and develop, but it also would have likely failed to wow potential donors.

**By Delivery Medium**—Like we did with Project Buddy, you could release iterations of a project by how it will be delivered, typically starting with the simplest to develop, so that the team learns early what works and what doesn't. ILT and vILT are often chosen as earlier iterations, saving e-learning and more complex media like virtual reality for future iterations.

**By Device or Platform**—If your project will require additional development to reach multiple devices, screen sizes, or platforms, you can set your iterations to release for one platform at a time. In this approach, take time between each iteration to make updates to content or delivery as needed while you're under the hood.

**By Project Phase**—Some projects are easily broken into smaller phases of release based on any number of factors, including the overall business cycle or an organization-wide program schedule. These evolve by applying learning from the early released phases to the portions released later.

**By Level of Finish/Functionality**—Workable early iterations can be done in simple development tools—even paper!—to test with learners before investing in more sophisticated builds. For example, you can create an MVP for a video project using phone-camera video or even still images in early iterations. You can prototype software training in system documentation before committing to video walk-throughs or course content, allowing you to focus on the topics that people really struggle with. And you can create early iterations of virtual reality experiences with simple 360 video interactions in e-learning. In each of these cases, the point is to find mistakes early in the project wherever possible. (You won't find them all right away, so don't be frustrated!)

**By Language**—Whenever training will be delivered in multiple languages, it helps to aim to complete a full release in the primary language (often English) before translation and localization begins. This will allow you to find errors and make adjustments only once before rippling that version through all the translated versions. It also gives your translation team a finished version as a reference point for their work, which is always appreciated!

**By Audience**—The first released iteration of a project is almost always designed for the primary learner persona. Subsequent iterations can provide support (more, less, different) for the secondary personas that have different needs than the primary persona, incorporating what was learned in the first iteration into the additional work.

**By Release Schedule**—If you're developing training for a change of some sort in the organization, you might iterate by learner populations with different needs. For example, if you're implementing a new software, you might start with the people who use the current system or process and need to make the change from old to new. This population is often further divided into subgroups such as super-users and occasional users, by functional distinction, and so on depending on the project. On the other hand are the newcomers who don't have the reference point of the old way of doing things, and for whom a "what's new!" message is really irrelevant. These learners may also have the same subgroups as the existing audience.

At this point you may have realized that there are often several approaches to iterations that run concurrently throughout a project. For example, nearly every project uses the alpha > beta > final approach in addition to a phased by-module or by-language or other approach.

A large multi-module project may have a staggered start approach where the implementation and evaluation part of one module feeds into the analysis work being done on the next module (Figure 9-2).

Similarly, a project that is releasing iterations by platform or by language may have a structure that resembles the example in Figure 9-3, where each section or language is developed fully—and learned from—before beginning the next.

**Figure 9-2.** A Project With Staggered Start Dates for Different Components

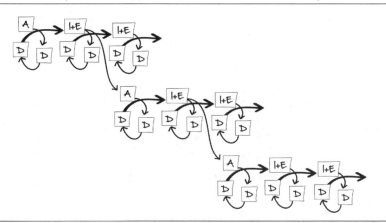

**Figure 9-3.** A Three-Phase Project of Iterations

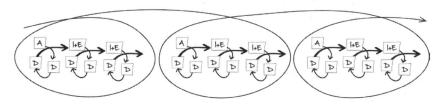

# What Should You Measure and When?

In a typical Agile instructional design project, the team has multiple opportunities to measure and evaluate, because the iterative development process builds in a feedback loop. Ideally, you can measure many of the same things during development and evaluation of each iteration that you plan to measure with the completed, released project.

This is ideal—and idealistic—because:

- During the project, it might not be feasible to see the full results of the training's effect on performance.
- Many instructional designers feel that the post-release evaluation of their programs is somewhat lacking.

Even so, the team can look closely at the learner experience with each iterative review cycle during project development. Depending on how you're collecting measurement and evaluation data (online surveys, reports from managers, xAPI), this is an excellent opportunity to answer detailed questions, such as whether learners think the information is conveyed clearly, whether managers see performance improvement from their employees, and where many learners pause or abandon an e-learning video.

Knowing this information can be valuable during the development process and over time and experience with the program.

## What Could Possibly Go Wrong?

Common issues with iterations include:

**You do not get actual *user* input.** It's well worth your while to work hard to get as close to actual learners as you can for your iteration reviews.

**You over-rely on reviews of design documents, project charters, or templates.** While perhaps useful to the project team, they are not workable products that can be used by a person to learn anything about the topic at hand.

**You wait too long before getting learners involved.** As soon in the process as you can, include learners or close proxies in the review cycle to determine if the learning solution actually works.

## Key Takeaways

- The iterative and incremental approach taken on an Agile project allows the development team to learn early on in the project timeline what works and what needs more work before it can be released.
- While SMEs, project sponsors, stakeholders, and other instructional designers offer a lot of insight in each review

cycle, members of the learner population are the ones who can really test if the deliverables help them do their jobs better.

- There are many ways to iterate within a project. The kickoff session is a good time to be talking about how this will take place on the project.

# CHAPTER 10

# Create Planning and Working Rhythms

In This Chapter
- What project rhythms does an Agile team use to keep the project on track?
- What is the purpose of creating rhythms for planning or for iterations?
- How do Agile teams work with SMEs?
- How can instructional design teams work with software development teams using Agile?

A recent project, Project Wingman, called for us to design and deliver 90 minutes of virtual classroom training in a week and a half's time. At the same time, the underlying business scope of the project was under constant evolution as the client team moved toward their release date. Here's how it went:

**Monday:** Kick off project with project sponsor's proxy.

**Wednesday:** Deliver project skeleton in morning, a high-level outline of content and ideas for activities thrown into a rough PowerPoint.

Meet to review with the rest of the client team in the evening to discuss needed changes. At this meeting, the nature of the messaging changed somewhat.

**Friday:** Deliver project alpha draft in morning, with the specific wording of key messages and activity definitions. Meet with the rest of the client team in the evening to discuss needed changes, including with the graphic designer for a preview of the graphics that would need to be created. We received further clarification about the changes that were being implemented from the business, and these were worked into the next version.

**Monday:** Deliver project beta draft in morning. (For this high-priority project, we worked over the weekend.) For this iteration, talking points and activity directions were moved off the PowerPoint slide and into the notes, freeing the slide for graphics. By the time we reached the review meeting time with the team, the business realized that they were providing training too soon in the project, and right now they wanted to focus on communications. The project was closed.

These short iterations and frequent reviews helped us all build on the prior iterations, allowed us to make adjustments early and often, and helped the client understand the degree of change  they were asking their people to make and actually slow down the training process accordingly. Rather than deliver a product at the end, spanning weeks or months of development, the client reached this decision early on thanks to the iterative cycle.

You've planned your project, estimated tasks, and designed your iterations. So now what? Just start working? As this story shows, the work itself is just half the equation. The other half is how you keep the flow going.

Agile teams have several planning and working rhythms that keep things moving with a predictable cadence and more or less steady flow of work. In this chapter we'll discuss weekly (or biweekly) planning meetings and iteration reviews. We'll also address unique scheduling options for instructional design teams that support software development teams using Agile.

## Rhythms for Weekly or Biweekly Planning

LLAMA teams meet weekly or biweekly for planning, depending on the size and volume of the project and the length of each iteration. These meetings provide a full-team look at the work ahead, balancing resources and team roles as needed and communicating the results in regular status reporting. Meetings include the entire team staffed on the project in the coming week or two (which means that most people have several planning meetings to attend). Regular planning meetings can cover six topics:

- **Overall project update:** The project lead gathers any metrics needed to be discussed, including a report of hours (if you're tracking them) and a comparison to the project's estimate. Any information updates or changes from the client are shared here (unless they were urgent enough to have been communicated as they came in). And finally, the team reviews work accomplished in the prior period to be included on the status report.

- **Week ahead planning:** This is generally the largest part of the meeting and includes the whole team working together to plan for the week (to reach an iteration milestone or complete some key tasks). Once goals for the week are set and understood, team members identify the tasks required to accomplish those goals and the hours estimated to complete them (see chapter 8 for identifying and estimating tasks). Any tasks or needs from the project sponsor or reviewers or from others who are not on the project team are also reviewed, such as what outside vendors or internal resources are needed to support the team in the near future. Finally, team members raise any personal scheduling and availability notes that affect this project. It might be that work on another project will prevent a team member from working as much on this project as planned, or that material expected from a SME has not yet arrived so work on another project can be pulled ahead in the intervening time.

- **Looking ahead:** The project manager and the team look at the remainder of the project's timeline, adjusting based on current project status and timeline. What needs will the team have from the project sponsor, from reviewers, or from others outside the team? Have any of these dates or commitments changed? If there are concerns about the team's ability to reach certain milestones on time (or if the team can meet them earlier), these are noted as issues to review with the project sponsor.

- **Risk management:** The risks identified for the project are reviewed in this meeting. Do any new mitigation efforts need to be made? Are there any new risks to the project's estimate, timeline, or scope? Do we feel we still have the right mix of team members and skills on the project? What constraints will the team face?

- **Expectations management:** Do the estimates for hours (effort) and timelines (duration) still match the expectations set at the beginning of the project? If so, what communication needs to happen with the project sponsor?

- **Reflecting:** Each week the team has the opportunity for a mini-retrospective, applying what is being learned as the project unfolds and making adjustments and improvements as needed. A simple start-stop-continue approach works well for this.

## Signs of a Poor Planning Meeting

- **The project manager does all the talking.** This is an opportunity for team members to contribute based on their own expertise.
- **The project manager defines and estimates all the tasks.** While the project manager certainly has insight into the activities that need to be completed, team members will be the ones doing their portion of the work and should contribute to the estimates.
- **The meeting doesn't happen.** A commitment to regular planning keeps the team on track. If the project manager cannot attend, the meeting can be rescheduled or held by team members. "The project manager didn't schedule a meeting" is no excuse for not planning!
- **Tasks do not get defined or estimated at a workable level.** Everyone should leave this meeting with a good enough sense for the tasks ahead to be able to start working.
- **Client is not updated after with results of the meeting.** While many project sponsors may not want all the detail that's covered in the weekly planning meeting, any regular status updates should be informed by the decisions made in the planning meetings.

# Rhythms for Iterations

Iterations themselves were discussed in chapter 9, but the team has an opportunity at each iteration review to reinforce the project rhythms in a deliberate way. One of the key aspects of an Agile project is the regularity and thoroughness with which each iteration is reviewed by SMEs, stakeholders, and actual learners or users. These review cycles can vary in their frequency and their duration.

- Let's take **frequency** first. For example, teams at TorranceLearning have found that a two-week cadence works well for a half-day's worth of (virtual) instructor-led training or 30-60 minutes of e-learning. That gives the team enough time to work in changes from the prior iteration and to incrementally advance the finish level of the deliverable. You might have some projects on very leisurely schedules, where content scope is the key project constraint, the SMEs are slow to deliver content and provide reviews, and everyone's expectation is that this project will move slowly. It might be one to two months between reviewable iterations. This can allow your team to slip this work in while they wait for other projects to pick up. On the other hand, intense, high-urgency, high-change projects might have iterations for review as frequently as every 48 hours, like Project Wingman.

- Similarly, iteration review **duration** can vary widely. This depends on who is reviewing a particular iteration (is it SMEs and stakeholders only or will actual learners and users be involved?) as that has a considerable impact on the length of time it will take them to review properly. Small and internal reviews may take as little as a few hours. Full user testing may take weeks or months to complete.

There is no right or wrong answer to the frequency and duration of iteration reviews. The key to planning them is to set good expectations and to communicate with the project sponsor when things aren't going as expected.

## What If the Weekly Task Breakdown and Estimate Are Out of Line With the Original Estimate?

This is where the proverbial rubber hits the road, and it's not always a comfortable place to be. First, check to confirm that your weekly tasks and estimates align with original estimates for the week or this stage of project. (Meaning, you may not be "off," you might just be ahead or behind.)

If you're indeed over your estimate or behind your timeline, here are some options to explore:

- Are there alternative approaches that could achieve the same goal?
- Get insight from the team and from the project sponsor to make sure that you're working on "must-have" tasks, and that "nice-to-have" tasks have not crept in.

- Determine if less should be done. Have you misunderstood the original desires for the project and you're over-delivering?
- Do nothing. As one of our early clients said, "It is what it is." Meaning, sometimes it just takes longer than you estimated it would. Remember, the only thing we know about an estimate is that it's wrong.

If you're significantly under your estimate or ahead of your timeline, you could:
- Do nothing. You may need this time or these hours later on. "It is what it is."
- Determine if more should be done. Have you misunderstood the original desires for the project and you're at risk for under-delivering?
- Celebrate! It's entirely possible that you'll be able to finish under estimate or ahead of schedule, freeing you and the team to deliver more later on.

# Working With Subject Matter Experts

Any great learning and development project has three key components: the content, the instructional design, and the media implementation. While your team is responsible for the instructional design and the media, most of the time you will rely on subject matter experts to provide the content, the portion of the project that you can't necessarily create yourself. You work closely with SMEs to better understand the content and to help with the nuance of the subject. That makes SMEs essential! They're also among the critical reviewers for a project, providing you with a valuable quality check for accuracy and completeness. And, they're a frequently cited reason why projects fail to deliver on time.

Most SMEs have a lot on their plate, and developing training is often not their highest priority. You must recognize that. Particularly when working with nonprofits and associations, SMEs are often volunteers. And the best SMEs are in high demand because of their expertise. In recognizing this, you should aim to meet them where they are. Each project will be unique, so you should work to find the best way to work with that project's SMEs. Here are a few examples of things you can do to accommodate SMEs:

- **Make sure you have the right SMEs.** That includes not only people with the required knowledge (of the subject and the learners) but also the time available for this project.
- **Flex your project timelines** around the schedules of SMEs wherever feasible and when this meets the needs of the project sponsor.
- **Meet them where they are.** Be flexible with how SMEs provide their information to you—whether you sit in on a class or webinar, read their book, interview them, accept a whitepaper, or job shadow them. One size does not fit all.
- **Ask carefully.** Don't ask them to give you everything they know (which can be a lot!) but rather the focused pieces that the learner needs. Sometimes this means going out, doing your own research, and bringing back something for the SME to review instead of having to start from scratch.
- **Plan ahead.** This approach to project management means that you can provide your SMEs with a timeline that works for them and a sense for how much time they'll need to participate in the process so they can plan. And as always, you must meet your commitments to be ready when they are.

How do you then motivate SMEs to participate in the instructional design process? There are a number of reasons why SMEs may be reluctant to share information, each one of which requires a different approach depending on the reason and the circumstances (volunteers versus employees versus consultants). Two of the most common reasons that SMEs don't share information freely is the availability of their time and the perceived loss of status (or actual loss of income) by giving up knowledge.

If the SME does not have enough time, you could:

- Wait until the SME has time (change the order of delivery of modules, for example).

- Compensate or otherwise incentivize the SME to move this project to a higher priority.
- Do outside research and bring the SME something to correct versus something to start from scratch.
- Work with a junior SME to get a lot of the early legwork completed, then finish with the senior SME.
- Attend a course on this topic that the SME was already giving.
- Work with the SME's leaders to reprioritize their workload accordingly.
- Get a team of SMEs.
- Get a different SME.

If the SME fears that by providing information, they will be giving up status, influence, or an income source, you could:

- Compensate the SME for the intellectual property.
- Give credit to the SME within or at the end of the course for their contribution.
- Ensure that this course that you're building is the first step toward a higher-level course to be offered by the SME.
- Ensure that what you teach in the course helps the SME manage their time by not having to field simple questions repeatedly.

As you can see, you're in this together with your SMEs—it's not an adversarial relationship at all! You must be appreciative of the SMEs you work with (and repeatedly let them know!) and incredibly respectful of their time.

## Aligning Rhythms With an Agile Software Team

In some cases, your training and development team will be supporting a software development team that uses Agile. When this happens, you'll want to align your planning, working, and iteration rhythms with the software team's so that you're not at odds. I've seen this done in several ways:

- **Work in line together:** The learning team's user stories (covered in chapter 5) are included among the software team's stories. This means that in order for the whole team to be successful, the software team must spend time on both development and training support. This can be effective, or it can risk development schedules.

- **Work staggered one (or more) software sprints behind:** The training team works on completed software one sprint after it's been developed (during testing) or one sprint after the testing is completed. This tends not to slow down the development team and, in some cases, the training team can be identifying software issues in the course of their work.

- **Ignore the software team's sprints and prioritize training development based on user needs:** Instead of chasing the software team, look at what features can be used without training and what ones cause issues for users, focusing your development there.

Whichever method you choose, know that software developed and released iteratively will be constantly changing. This offers the training teams a number of built-in opportunities for developing and learning iteratively as new features are released regularly.

## What Could Possibly Go Wrong?

Common issues with project rhythms include:

**Teams with variable rhythms can face confusion about schedules and priorities.** In an environment of near-constant change, the rhythm and ritual of Agile is one of the few things your team can count on.

**You skip planning rhythms when schedules are tight.** When schedules and budgets are tight, these are exactly the times when planning is most critical.

**You skip planning rhythms when iterations are infrequent.** It can be tempting to lighten up on planning when the project sponsor doesn't seem to be in a big hurry. Unfortunately, I've seen these projects eat up hours and timeline without noticing.

## Key Takeaways

- Set a rhythm! Plan and adjust when you need to according to project needs; these are not rigid rules.
- Working flexibly with SMEs is the best way to leverage their time productively and constructively in the project.
- Rhythms for training teams supporting Agile software teams need to be intentional and aligned with the software development schedule.

# CHAPTER 11

# Maintain Regular, Open Lines of Communication

**In This Chapter**
- How do you communicate the status of an Agile project?
- To whom do you communicate?

We once worked with a project sponsor who usually asked us to do very small, very limited in scope, and very tight-on-budget projects. We knew his resources were limited, and we did our best to help him out wherever we could.

As part of a request to make some additions to an existing curriculum, he asked if we could save him some time and money on Project Northstar by "just skipping all that status tracking and reporting stuff that you do. You could just focus on getting the work done."

> Just focus on getting the work done.

I replied that a project with a tight timeline and a tight budget like this was exactly the kind of project that needed status tracking and reporting the most so that we could collectively be on top of issues before they got big . . . and expensive.

One of the hallmarks of a successful Agile project team is the transparency of communication, often seen in frequent status check-ins with project sponsors, SMEs, and stakeholders. Open and honest communication in the face of fast-moving, iterating, and changing projects are essential. This is an opportunity to communicate and document officially the status of the project as well as to get quick feedback and insight as to how best to resolve issues that the project team has encountered. In many cases, particularly in the early weeks of a project, you are already communicating with the project sponsor and with subject matter expert on a regular basis and not waiting until status communications to raise issues. Even when you are communicating daily or more frequently about specific tactical issues, the high-level status report provides context for the entire project effort as it is moving forward. It is also possible that your day-to-day communications do not involve the project sponsor, so the formal status communication is incredibly effective in keeping that person in the loop on what is going on in the project.

While every project has its own unique needs and rhythm, for LLAMA projects I recommend you communicate status in two ways: in written format and in a meeting (whether face-to-face, via phone, or via video conference).

## Written Status Reports

Written status reports have the benefit of not only conveying your content but also documenting the project at a point of time in case you need to refer back to decisions made or communications that were sent. You can use them to set the stage for the work to come by sending status reports at the beginning of each week. Status reports include a high-level summary of the project followed by lists of the tasks that were completed in the last week and tasks planned to be completed in the coming week by the business team and the project team.

Similar to the color-coding with the project plan visuals, you might also document any open issues that need resolution by the impact on the team's progress if they are not resolved in the coming week. For example:

- **Green:** does not hinder our progress in the coming week.
- **Orange:** could hinder our progress in the coming week.
- **Red:** we are on full stop and cannot progress without resolution of the issue.

## Example Status Report

This is an actual project status report for a project code named LACQUER that had two modules. Status reports were sent weekly on Monday. We also set up a weekly conference call update to further discuss issues, ideas, and status.

### Overview

LS and Combo Alpha storyboards and the LACQUER Self beta v2 have been delivered for review. We'll begin implementing feedback next week with an eye toward beginning the beta build for LS and Combo and finalizing the LACQUER Self.

### Tasks Completed Last and This Week

- Incorporated SME feedback into LACQUER Self beta v2
- Simplified Gerard scenario
- Broke long video into smaller chunks
- Designed knowledge checks for each video chunk
- Added visuals and functionality descriptions to alpha storyboards
- Confirmed/clarified understanding of LS

### Tasks to Be Completed Next Week

- Read through reviewer's comments and ask for any clarification if necessary (all three modules).
- Convert SME feedback into tasks for course builders (all three modules).

- Revise VO scripts and send to artist for final recording (LACQUER Self).
- Begin beta build (LS and Combo).
- Begin final iteration (LACQUER Self).

**Open Issues/Questions**
- Do you know when you'll have KR's opening video for LACQUER Self? (And we left it that you're editing, correct?)
- I'm working on estimating how much more will be invoiced this year. Do you just need to know for this year or for the remainder of the projects?
- We didn't officially determine how the additional beta cycle will affect the LACQUER Self delivery. Here's what I'm thinking. If this works for you, I can update the workplan, or we can chat about it during our next phone call.

**Estimate to Actuals**
**LACQUER Self:** We're still well below the estimate, which is helpful because we added another review cycle to this project. Even with the extra review cycle, I'm hopeful that we'll complete this project without needing the contingency.

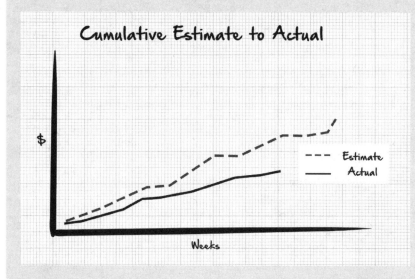

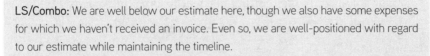

**LS/Combo:** We are well below our estimate here, though we also have some expenses for which we haven't received an invoice. Even so, we are well-positioned with regard to our estimate while maintaining the timeline.

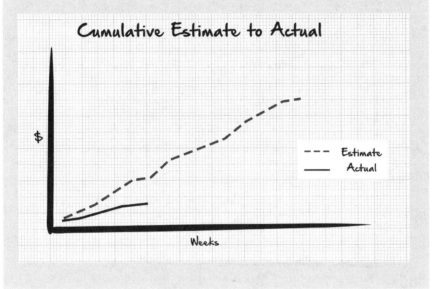

The last piece of our status report is probably the one most interesting to our clients. It is where we share our cumulative actual hours spent against the estimate for the project that was set when we started out. This is the visual that puts the entire project status into context: Are you ahead of schedule or behind? Are you spending more or less time or money than planned?

Each week you can add to the spreadsheet of estimated hours or cost (depending on what is most important to your client) of what was actually incurred for that week, and provide some commentary about why you are where you are. Figures 11-1 to 11-5 present a few charts offering different project status updates. These are expressed in dollars (most important to TorranceLearning's clients), but an internal project team may choose to express their charts in hours instead.

When a project is just getting started, it looks like Figure 11-1. We see the entire plan for the hours for the project, but the actual line is just starting out.

**Figure 11-1.** Project Just Starting Out

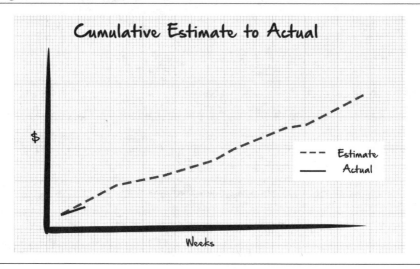

**Figure 11-2.** Project Progressing Faster Than Estimated

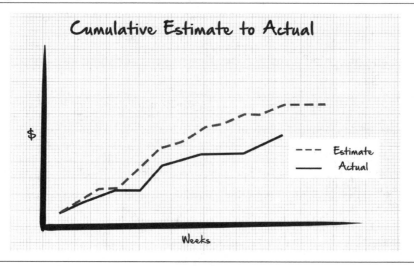

Figure 11-2 is an example of a project that is incurring fewer hours than we estimated it would. It's the kind of graph that makes everyone happy.

Figure 11-3 is one in which more hours were incurred than estimated in the early weeks, but held pretty close to the estimates from there on out. In this case the project finished ahead of schedule and under the estimate: The actual (solid) line ends earlier than the estimate (dashed) line, and is lower than the estimate projected for the end of the project.

**Figure 11-3.** Project Started Out Behind Schedule Before Catching Up

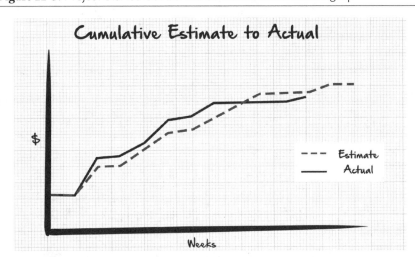

Figure 11-4 shows a project that was working along under its estimate until a big chunk of hours or expenses hit mid-project where the actual line crosses the estimate, pushing it over the estimate and right up to its top amount, even before finishing.

**Figure 11-4.** Project Started Out Under Estimate, Then Went Over

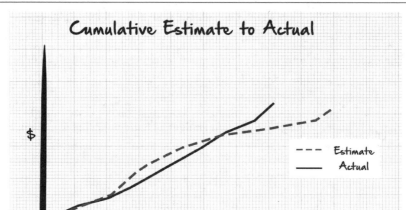

In Figure 11-5, the client took far longer to get iteration reviews completed so the entire graph is stretching out to the right as additional weeks are added in.

**Figure 11-5.** Project Extended Due to Review Delays

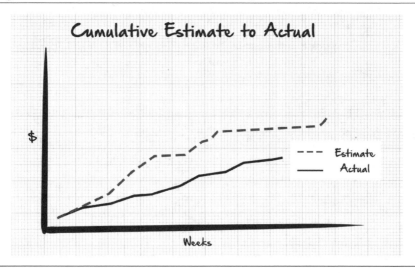

While the graphs are certainly eye-catching, what's more interesting and useful is the story behind the shape of each line. There's no good or bad to the lines in and of themselves; whether or not the actual line is above or below the original estimate is only part of the picture. What's important is the trajectory of the project and how things are going. For a project in which you are able to work faster than estimated (or in which you were requested to do more than you were originally, and you are authorized to spend the hours to do so) it's perfectly OK to have the actual line be above the estimate line. Or, in a project in which contact experts or reviewers are slow to respond, you may be below the estimated hourly cost line simply because you have not yet had the work to do.

## Status and Review Meetings

While the status report documents a point in time for the project, regular status and review meetings are working sessions in which issues are tackled, deliverables in progress are shared and reviewed, and the project team gets insight from the project sponsor and vice versa. Agile software teams hold regular sprint review meetings with their product owners. At these meetings, the work that has been previously completed is demonstrated and the new work plan for the next sprint ahead is reviewed.

A LLAMA status update meeting is similar. And, of course, you should add a few things. Of note, start with the question, "What has changed since we last talked?" On most projects it is entirely possible that several things have changed since the previous status meeting that the project sponsor has not had an opportunity or thought to communicate to the project team. By opening a meeting with this question, you convey to the project sponsor that you expect that things will change and that you're OK with this—you just want to know about it.

# The Status Reporting Rhythm

On a typical project you might have each of these types of status communication occur weekly. On faster moving projects it's advisable to check in via phone or in person more frequently than weekly; on slower moving projects you may not get together quite so often.

For some projects the weekly written status report and the weekly meeting happen on the same day or on adjacent days. This makes it easy to handle any questions about the estimate-to-actual graph that may come up and you can quickly resolve the issues that were identified in the status report. Keeping the two types of communication together works well for project sponsors who tend not to respond quickly via email.

On other projects you can send the written status report on Monday and schedule a Wednesday or Thursday live check-in meeting. This works particularly well with clients who are speedy to respond via email, and gives you two opportunities a week to check in on the overall project status and resolve issues. For projects that are very fast moving, you may schedule additional status meetings as needed.

# Whom to Communicate With?

On our first status report, we ask the project sponsor whom they would like to include in the communications. For the written status report, we often include the project sponsor, any proxy or project manager designated by the project sponsor as a frequent point of contact, and sometimes key SMEs or stakeholders. It's important that the project team also see the status reports that go out to the clients even if they don't have any direct contact with the client themselves. This provides the context they need in order to keep the clients' needs in mind as work is being performed.

With weekly update meetings, you may have a slightly smaller audience, with subject matter experts and stakeholders joining on an as-needed basis.

In these meetings, sometimes you will discuss the availability and priorities of the subject matter experts and the people that you need to work on your team.

## What Could Possibly Go Wrong?

A common issue with communicating status is:

**You skip status reports and status meetings to save money and time.** The single biggest point of failure is when you fail to communicate status, often requested by the project sponsor in an effort to save time, save resources, or "save you the trouble." The projects on which time and resources are tight are the very ones that need active management and communication through status reporting.

## Key Takeaways

- Communicate often in both written and meeting formats if you can. The written updates provide documentation and clarity, where the meeting formats allow for conversation around status, timelines, and decisions made along the way.
- Focus on activity and deliverables, not percentage of completion. An Agile project is measured in terms of delivered learning experiences.
- Tell the story behind the numbers. While the graphs and charts are nice "eye candy," the reasons why a project is over or under its estimate, or ahead of or behind its schedule, are more important.

# CHAPTER 12

# Facilitate Retrospectives

In This Chapter

∘ How do you incorporate learning cycles within and across projects?

∘ How do you capture lessons learned for use in later projects?

When the team has a million and one things going on, the retrospective can get forgotten in the fray. That happened on a large project with eight sizeable course modules to be designed and developed over a four-month period by a team of five people. With a staggered start for the modules (one or two started every week for the first five weeks of the project), each iteration rolled in after the next without an obvious pause to reflect. At three

I know it's crunch time ... but let's get retrospective on this.

months into the project, the team members' patience with each other and the project was fraying. It seemed like the same types of requests were getting made each week, module after module, with little to show for it. A retrospective was called.

At the time, it seemed a little crazy to stop the project since the deadline was looming and patience with meetings was already wearing thin. But the team got together and spent several hours dissecting and refining their process, airing their grievances, and hammering out a path forward. They identified ways to improve the current project and recommended changes in our overall processes for the next time. Things were still a bit tense but workable.

Several months later, a subset of the members of that team were on another project together and just getting started. Several first and second iteration deliverables were out with the client for review, there was a pause in the action, and the team lead called a retrospective. This time the retrospective was greeted with more enthusiasm. The short reflection generated a few ideas to make things work better on this project, and the team felt relieved to have the structure for a frank conversation about process, not personality.

Retrospectives work better when you have more of them, have them frequently, and when you don't "need" them.

Agile project management focuses on improvement. All too often in our work as L&D professionals, we don't find the time to stop and reflect on our own learning and improvement. And yet, each project and each iteration holds the opportunity for learning. The rhythms of an Agile team offer opportunities to improve. And at the completion of each sprint and at the completion of a project, the team takes a look at the entire process. It's an Agile principle: "At regular intervals, the team reflects on how to become more effective then tunes and adjusts its behavior accordingly."

These regular cycles allow you to incorporate learning and improvement both within the project (what can we be doing better now?) and from project to project (what can we be doing better across the board?).

This meeting is called a "retrospective." The retrospective is intended for deliberate reflection on the team's processes and approach to the project, not the project's deliverable.

Here's a pro tip: Have your team keep a running list of issues and suggestions to raise in retrospectives. This helps your team keep from forgetting issues to discuss. A team member might jot down something that can help on the current project or on future projects. The running list can serve as the starting point for more formal team retrospective sessions.

## Who Participates in the Retrospective?

Many retrospectives are conducted with only team members, not the sponsor or SMEs. This allows the team the freedom to be more transparent about what went well and what didn't go well. Of course, there are many good reasons to include these other key roles in a "lessons learned" session; however, that should not replace the need for the team to reflect within itself.

Depending on the team's needs, the retrospective can be facilitated by one of several people:

- **The project manager:** This is a convenient choice since the project manager (ostensibly you) will be invited and has led the project to date. However, this makes it difficult for the project manager to participate fully and equally as a team member.
- **A peer project manager or the project manager's leader:** This is a great option as it allows for someone with the experience of leading a team—but not this team—and experienced in leading retrospectives to facilitate the conversation, freeing the team's leader to participate. This option also starts the process of organizational learning by exposing others to the team's improvement process.

• **A professional facilitator or Agile coach:** Sometimes having an outsider lead the retrospective allows everyone to participate fully. The expert facilitator can draw on his or her experience across many retrospectives to help the team.

## Agenda for the Retrospective

A common format for this meeting is the tried and true start-stop-continue. An example of a project team's retrospective using this format is in Figure 12-1.

Each member of the team identifies things that the team should:

• start doing
• stop doing
• continue doing.

Other questions the team could ask include finding out from each team member what was:

• enjoyable
• frustrating
• puzzling
• a moment of pride
• embarrassing.

And, for the next sprint or project, what they want to do:

• more of
• less of
• to the same extent.

(This last item is a lot like start-stop-continue.)

The retrospective might identify ways to improve the approach to working on the specific project or ways for the team overall to become more effective, more efficient, better communicators, and so on.

# Keep the Retrospective Constructive and Forward-Looking

Often the most challenging part of the retrospective, aside from allocating the time to have one, is keeping it constructive and forward-looking. This is, of course, especially challenging on a project that has had more than its share of challenges.

Everyone—not just the facilitator—has a part to play in keeping retrospectives positive. Note that these are called "retrospectives" and not "blaming sessions" or "scapegoat identification workshops." The goal of the retrospective needs to be focused on learning and improvement. As soon as it turns to blame and punishment, they cease to support learning.

There are several steps you can take to keep retrospectives positive:

- Start with what went well on the project before turning to the problems. Take care to find lessons learned in the positive to set the stage, especially if you know there are significant negatives to be addressed.
- Focus on the learning that the team can take forward, with only as much detailed dissection of the problem areas as is necessary. Often the historical facts matter less than the lessons to be learned from the situation.
- Admit your own mistakes and what can be learned from them.
- Conduct retrospectives on all projects, not just the ones that experience difficulties. That way "doing a retrospective" doesn't become synonymous with "this one went bad."
- Remind participants that feedback should be relevant and useable for others who might review it later. The retrospective should still make sense to people not on the project.

**Figure 12-1.** Notes From an E-Learning Project's Retrospective

### Proud Moments
When we were able to improve the client's video pacing, turning it from an awkward moment of failure into a demonstration of what we're able to do with our skills.

When the client's executive sponsor called Megan to discuss strategic organization changes not directly related to the project—a sign of trust and collaboration.

### Embarrassed Moments
In the Ignition (kickoff) we promised access to Trello—then forgot to provide it. They only asked for it much later on in the project, when the people in the Ignition session had already forgotten it. We honestly feel this is too much detail for the average client to share and would not recommend offering it in the future.

Graphics and animations were over-polished at beta stage. This then made it harder to change later.

### Budget/Timeline
Project is over budget because the underlying software was changing (unexpectedly at that point) as we were developing training. Lots of communication about it, starting early in the project status updates. Client willing to pay for requested changes because they were needed.

| START | STOP | CONTINUE |
|---|---|---|
| Consider recording working sessions done via online tools | Offer invitations to Trello | Offer new ways of collaboration, like getting on a video conference to do it in detail side-by-side. |
| Create standards earlier for the course/ curriculum/client (see to-do item) | Resist the urge to bake in hard-to-change features in the beta draft when we know things are in constant flux–it's just too time-consuming to undo later if that piece changes | Get together with client to get feedback in real time instead of handing it over the wall. (Agile principle: The best communication is face to face.) |

| START | STOP | CONTINUE |
|---|---|---|
| Increase the team's Camtasia knowledge so that we're not single-threading through one person or ruining her vacations (see to-do item) | | Communicate the estimate-to-actuals graph in status reports; this was a life-saver in sharing the impacts of late software changes on our work and approaching it collaboratively. |

### To-Do Items

For whole dev team: Define the list of standards most courses should have and add to OneNote for use by future teams.

LG: Look into Camtasia training for rest of team—what's the best option?

# Implementing Changes Identified in the Retrospective

Three types of action items come out of retrospectives, each with their own appropriate follow-up:

- **Individual action items:** A task that an individual takes on to improve their own skills or to implement for the rest of the team. Examples include learning about a particular technique or piece of software (personal learning) or performing a specific task like adding files to a project, communicating something with the project sponsor, or making a specific purchase.
- **Project team action items:** These are typically found during mid-project retrospectives and involve the project team implementing something learned in the retrospective. Examples include following a new process or changing the way that the team communicates with the client.
- **Organizational action items:** These are the most powerful action items and often have the most impact. These come from

lessons learned by the team that can be shared or addressed in a forum larger than the team itself. Someone in the retrospective is then tasked with taking this forward to that larger forum so it can be addressed there.

## What Could Possibly Go Wrong?

Common issues with retrospectives include:

**You don't hold a retrospective.** Don't make the mistake of believing that they're not needed or assuming that everyone has already raised any pertinent issues.

**You focus too much on the wrong things.** Don't fall into the trap of worrying about what won't ever happen again rather than emphasizing concrete suggestions for improving the process.

**You do not document the needed next steps.** It's important that you take stock of any issues and move them to the appropriate forum to get resolved. Otherwise what the team learns won't be shared and used across the organization.

## Key Takeaways

- Hold a retrospective after each iteration. Learn from them. Hold one at the end of the project too.
- Consider using an outside facilitator (another manager or a professional facilitator) to enable the project manager to participate freely in the retrospective.
- Keep retrospectives blame-free and future-focused to encourage learning and openness.

# Part 3.
## Applying Agile in Your Organization

# CHAPTER 13

# Scaling Agile

A few years ago one of our senior instructional designers took a well-earned vacation with her husband to Cancun. We had plenty of advance notice, and she had planned her project timelines around her vacation so that there'd be no disruptions.

Unfortunately, on the morning Sue was due to fly back, I got an email from her husband. As it turns out, while dancing on the beach on the last night of their vacation, Sue fell and broke her ankle horribly. She would be coming back late, with 13 pins in her ankle and a month of pain medication that would render her clearly "unfit for duty" at the office.

Surprise! Sue's not coming in to work for a month.

We called a meeting of our project managers to our LEGO board where we keep track of projects and people's assignments for a rolling six-week period. Within a short bit we had reallocated Sue's work to other people, and we knew which weeks we were going to be tight on resources.

A physical, visual system in which we were able to make decisions and see their impacts made this process go a lot more smoothly!

Up until this point we've been looking at Agile with a single team on a single project. Most organizations will have several—or many—team members and projects going on at the same time. This chapter will provide a number of techniques for managing in that more realistic and more complex environment.

In many respects the core question in any multiproject environment is what to work on in what order. Your organization's culture and needs will play a significant part in this decision. Agile principles offer some insights. Let's take these two principles to start with:

- Deliver working software [learning experiences] frequently, from a couple of weeks to a couple of months, with a preference to the shorter timescale.
- Working software [learning experiences] is the primary measure of progress.

Taken together, these two principles will guide you and your team to have as much focused time on as few as possible projects to get them finished and delivered. This often strikes people as counter-intuitive, so let's consider a hypothetical situation. Your team has been tasked with completing 12 projects in one year. You estimate that each project happens to have exactly the same work effort required to complete them: four weeks each, which is about 32 hours/week x 4 = 128 hours of effort.

For the sake of argument, assume that there is no waiting period for SMEs or reviewers. (That's clearly unrealistic, so I'll get to that in a bit.) You could work on one project a month and your work would look something like the timeline in Figure 13-1. Surely the people who want projects nine, 10, 11, and 12 may be frustrated to have to wait for you to get around to their projects.

**Figure 13-1.** Twelve Projects, One a Month

| JAN | FEB | MAR | APR | MAY | JUN | JUL | AUG | SEP | OCT | NOV | DEC |
|-----|-----|-----|-----|-----|-----|-----|-----|-----|-----|-----|-----|
| Project 1 | Project 2 | Project 3 | Project 4 | Project 5 | Project 6 | Project 7 | Project 8 | Project 9 | Project 10 | Project 11 | Project 12 |

Another approach is to work a little bit on all the projects in every month. This approach would surely show that you are serious about getting this work done because you've started right away on everything! If you plotted out the work for the year, your timeline would look something like Figure 13-2.

**Figure 13-2.** Twelve Projects, All at Once

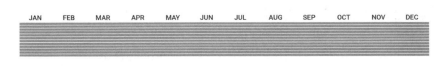

| JAN | FEB | MAR | APR | MAY | JUN | JUL | AUG | SEP | OCT | NOV | DEC |
|-----|-----|-----|-----|-----|-----|-----|-----|-----|-----|-----|-----|

In this plan, you won't have a releasable finished product for *any* of the 12 projects until the end of December, whereas in the month-by-month, one-project-at-a-time-approach you are at releasing workable and usable product each month. In the monthly plan, the average wait time to deliver is six months, with some projects waiting less and some waiting more. In the everything-at-once approach, the average is 12 months before any work is delivered! Doing a little bit of everything all at the same time actually means that the organization has to wait longer for output.

In most organizations, some projects will be ready to go right away, and others won't be ready or can wait. By working on the highest priority projects first, and as few projects at a time as possible, the delivery schedule and the organization are kept happy.

Of course, working on just one project at a time isn't usually feasible because you'll often find yourself waiting on others, such as SMEs, reviewers, leaders, and media production. Having a small number of projects going on at any given time is generally more feasible and sustainable. An oversimplified look at this overlapping of projects could look like Figure 13-3, where each project is broken into three iterations with a month of implementation and evaluation in between each iteration.

**Figure 13-3.** Twelve Projects, Broken Into Iterations

| JAN | FEB | MAR | APR | MAY | JUN | JUL | AUG | SEP | OCT | NOV | DEC |
|-----|-----|-----|-----|-----|-----|-----|-----|-----|-----|-----|-----|
| 1 | 4 | 1 | 4 | 1 | 4 | 7 | 10 | 7 | 10 | 7 | 10 |
| 2 | 5 | 2 | 5 | 2 | 5 | 8 | 11 | 8 | 11 | 8 | 11 |
| 3 | 6 | 3 | 6 | 3 | 6 | 9 | 12 | 9 | 12 | 9 | 12 |

This fully supports the iterative nature of an Agile project. With this approach, the average time to completion of any project is nine months, with the earliest releases taking five months and being available in May. Assuming, of course, that you have a reasonable estimate of the work that will be entailed on any one project, you can prioritize the projects at hand, and you can determine whether you have the resources to complete them, either internally or externally.

## Managing Team Resources

At the same time that you're planning projects, you need to be assigning people to teams and managing their overall time spent. While not explicitly an Agile-informed process, you can ensure that you are smoothing the effort expected from each person while making sure that projects have the right team members at the right time, informed by the Agile principle: "Agile processes promote sustainable development. The sponsors, developers, and users should be able to maintain a constant pace indefinitely."

At TorranceLearning, we use a large board of LEGOs laid out like a big, colorful spreadsheet to organize our resource planning (Figure 13-4).

**Figure 13-4.** Using LEGOs to Manage Team Resources

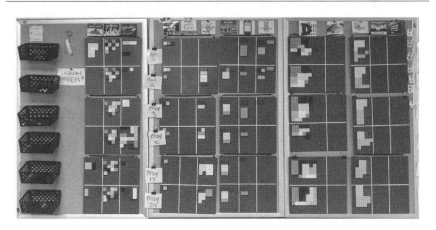

In this scheme, each project is shown in a single column, and each row across represents a week. We plan our resources out six weeks at a time, rotating the dates on the board every two weeks to keep this fresh. Every week our project leads get together to "do the LEGOs." Here's how it works:

- Each team member has a LEGO color.
- A standard 2x4 rectangular brick has eight bumps which correspond nicely to a full eight-hour day of work. It takes five rectangular bricks to represent a full-time week. (Note that we don't actually schedule 40 hours in a week of project time. This is just a rough approximation of project staffing, not a detailed schedule.)

- Team members who have alternate appointments or don't work a full-time schedule start out each week with a smaller number of rectangular bricks.
- Since this is just a broad brush look at resource allocation, we only deal with 2x4 rectangles and 2x2 square bricks (representing a half day).
- We start out each week with all the LEGOs in the bin on the far left of the big board.
- When teammates are out of the office on vacation or on a trip, those bricks go in the first column on the board and cannot be pulled onto projects.
- Our second column is for keeping track of those inevitable office communications, staff meetings, and other valuable things that need to be done but reduce the time available for working on projects.
- After that, all other bricks (hours) remaining can be spread across the project columns according to project needs.
- Wherever a project does not have the needed resources, we flag it for discussion and resolution.

This results in a visual and tactile representation of the work going on and resource needs across the projects. It prevents us from overloading or underloading people and is a transparent look at workloads across the team. And, when something happens on a project or in a teammate's work schedule, we're able to instantly see what gaps need to be filled.

## Prioritizing Projects

Nothing is ever as neat and tidy as they are when described in a book. The real world is much messier and there are two questions that come to mind when dealing with the realities of prioritizing projects and assigning team members' time:

- Which projects should we plan to go first?
- What happens when there are conflicts?

To resolve project scheduling conflicts, we use a project prioritization process that's easy to follow. First, all projects are given a priority score. In some organizations, projects are force-ranked from 1 to *n*. Other teams find that a simple score is sufficient in most cases and just assign scores with the high scores indicating higher priority projects. The point is to make it clear to everyone which projects have higher priority than others.

Then, when there is a conflict about what task should be worked on next or which team can pull extra resources from what other teams, there are four simple rules:

- Do the critical path project work first—these tasks are the ones that will put a project's timeline in jeopardy or hold others up from doing their work if they are not done.
- If both tasks are on the critical path, work on the higher priority project's critical path task first.
- If neither task is on the critical path, work on the task with the shorter time estimate first to keep things moving.
- Communicate changes that are made to projects timelines and resourcing as appropriate.

Each organization will have different criteria by which they score their projects for prioritization, with the biggest difference being between teams that work internal to an organization and teams that serve many different clients. (Some sample criteria are in the following sidebar.) Once scored, the project's prioritization also informs the organization about how many projects can be undertaken at any one time or when and whether outside resources or more team members may be required.

## Sample Project Prioritization Criteria for Internal L&D Teams

- **Organizational Strategy:** Does this project directly support key organizational strategies?
- **Deadline:** Are there firm, published, critical release deadlines for this project?
- **People Growth:** Does this project allow us to grow our people's skills in a way that will make them more capable in the future?
- **Politics:** Is this project a high visibility or high priority project for a leader?
- **Multiplier Effect:** Is this project one that will enable other projects in the future?
- **Volume:** Does this project impact a large number of people?
- **Regulatory or Legal:** Is this training required to meet a regulatory or legal requirement and therefore not at all optional? Is it triggered by an audit or survey finding?

## Sample Project Prioritization Criteria for External Teams Serving Multiple Clients

- **Deadline:** Does the client have firm, published, critical release deadlines for this project?
- **Margin:** Does this project bring a relatively large amount of margin to the company?
- **Relationship:** Do we have a longstanding relationship with this client? Do we foresee or desire one?
- **Loss Risk:** Are we at risk for losing this or future work if the project schedules slip?
- **People Growth:** Does this project allow us to grow our people's skills in a way that will make them more capable in the future?

# What Could Possibly Go Wrong?

Common issues with scaling Agile across multiple teams include:

**You are working on too many projects at once.** Having many things in progress stretches delivery dates, where focusing on a small number of projects at once provides quicker release of finished projects.

**You stretch team members too thin.** Whether you use LEGOs or online software or another tool, be sure that you have processes in place to prevent over (or under) scheduling team members.

**You aren't transparent about project prioritization.** Everything isn't equally important. If the organization cannot identify what work is most important, it's likely that the most important work won't get done.

## Key Takeaways

- Visual tools for resource management make it easy to see who's doing what and when and make it easy to see what needs to be adjusted when necessary.
- Work with project sponsors and leaders to identify criteria by which you can prioritize projects to make decision making transparent and drama-free (or at least less drama-filled).

# CHAPTER 14

# The Organizational Mindset Shift to Agile

**In This Chapter**
- How does the organizational culture create a supportive environment for Agile?
- How does Agile support constant change?
- How does Agile reduce waste in knowledge work such as instructional design?
- Why is trust so important in an organization that uses Agile?

A course developer after about six months on the job: "You really don't get it, do you? This place is weird. I mean, a wonderful kind of weird. But I've never worked in a place that works like this. I can't really explain it."

Me: [speechless]

"It" is the culture that supports and arises from a team that uses Agile, a culture built on transparency and remarkably low on drama. Oh, sure, we're all people and sometimes people get stressed out, say things that hurt, or make mistakes. But a culture that's truly supportive of Agile is supportive of people.

After a while I've realized that I no longer notice "it." Like a fish who doesn't notice that it's wet all the time, our team has become used to our culture and the way we work. It no  longer seems remarkable. It's not that we don't have room to improve—we're working on getting better all the time!—but we start in a pretty good place.

As you've read through this book, you might have noticed a common language describing Agile processes: There's a lot of emphasis on *people* and *trust: helping, individuals, interactions, collaboration.* Revisit the 12 founding Agile principles and you'll see even more: *customer, people, motivated individuals, support, face-to-face, teams, reflect.* The language around Agile makes it obvious that it requires the people in the organization to create a culture that supports these processes.

## Understanding Organizational Culture

Each organization has a unique culture that consists of the way people behave in that organization and the meanings that people in the organization assign to those behaviors. The culture refers to explicit and implicit aspects of the workplace, including the organization's values, norms, tools, language, habits, artifacts, and spaces. An organizational culture is "the way we do things around here." Your organization has its own culture, whether it's explicit or implicit.

Explicit aspects of an organizational culture can be written in the employee handbook or other policy documents. These might cover things as varied as working hours, how to order equipment, and a diversity policy.

The implicit aspects of culture are less visible. A newcomer will have to infer these from observation or ask colleagues about them. Implicit culture might govern communication preferences, management styles, degree of collaboration, or definitions of success. These concepts might not be articulated anywhere, but that doesn't make them any less important to consider.

Many Agile best practices fall into the "implicit" camp—they might be among those "in the air" cultural norms that aren't the sort you'd write in a manual or a list of rules. This can make it tricky to implement Agile or create an organizational culture that supports Agile project management.

Shifting to an Agile project management approach might lead to natural changes to your department's and your team's explicit and implicit culture; some of these changes might be essential to allow the Agile approach to work effectively. Most important is understanding how your organization communicates.

## Communication Is a Constant

Clear, open communication is at the heart of the Agile process. Frequent communication among team members is an obvious necessity. So is communication among project sponsors and project leads as well as between these key individuals and other team members. An Agile organizational culture must support frequent communication across organizational boundaries and between all levels of the organizational hierarchy.

## Communicate In Person

In this age of digital ease, Agile's communication principle can seem a bit of a throwback: It encourages face-to-face communication whenever possible. Ideally an Agile team holds a daily in-person (or at least synchronous) stand-up meeting. At these, team members literally stand in a circle and report on their progress, what's been completed, what they plan for that day, and whether there are any factors blocking their progress. The stand-up aspect helps ensure that meetings are short and focused (often only 15 minutes). Other, less formal communication is best done in person as well, whenever that is possible.

## Communicate Visually

A visual plan is a practical way to track a project and achieve constant, clear communication. With a planning board, whether it's physical or virtual, any team member or stakeholder can, at any time, get a quick status update at a glance.

The visual project plan makes it easy to communicate without interrupting teammates: Planning workflow and wondering whether another team member is available to help you? Check their board. Need to change the priority of a task? Reorder the cards.

## Communicate About Problems

The Agile project management process is ideal for instructional design projects—and most organizational projects, for that matter—in part because it can accommodate changes well as long as people communicate about problems and roadblocks as they arise. The daily stand-ups are the place to express concerns and warn of potential issues or delays. In addition, Agile teams use color-coding and notes on their planning boards as a way to show which tasks have issues.

### Reframe Success and Failure

One obstacle to clear communication and successful Agile project management is an organizational culture that equates problems with failure. To leverage the flexibility of Agile, it is essential to reframe success and, especially, failure. Managers and team members alike have to see problems as problems—problems that have solutions. This is a different mindset than seeing a problem as an irredeemable personal or organizational failure.

With a "failure" mindset, the person who discovers the problem might be tempted to hide knowledge of it; a manager might be tempted to assign blame.

If, instead, glitches are seen as fixable challenges, all hands can step in to creatively problem solve. When problems are seen as challenges to overcome, it suddenly becomes easier for everyone to communicate.

Solving a problem doesn't mean ignoring the cause. Once the project is back on track, the team should research the cause, identify any individual or organizational factors, and address them. Reflecting on and learning from problems is an integral element of Agile.

## Communicate With Stakeholders

Frequent communication benefits the organization, sure. It also benefits the stakeholders. Ideally, stakeholders are actively engaged with the Agile process. Send updates on progress, review tasks, and check in to ensure that all parties agree on project scope. Frequent, open communication helps prevent surprises like enormous changes in scope or focus late in the game.

Once your organization has built in the mechanisms to ensure constant communication—hopefully that's in-person with a visual component that's focused on identifying and solving problems as they arise, and that keeps everyone, including stakeholders, in the loop—you're one step closer to shifting the organizational culture in an Agile direction. In doing so, you also strengthen your organization's ability to manage and embrace change.

# Agile Embraces Change

In an Agile culture, change is welcomed. Rather than something to fear and avoid, change is seen as an inevitable part of an Agile project. Organizations are created to achieve large goals. To do this at scale, traditional organizations have created processes to foster consistency and reliability and to drive out variation. Yet in environments of increasing change and a mandate for creative solutions, organizations must embrace methods that are resilient in the face of constant change. The Agile process can only work if cultural practices within the organization support and embrace change.

The focus on rapid iteration means Agile teams can leverage change. Despite the historical connotation of Agile and rapid, embracing a project sponsor's change requests can mean moving more slowly. That's because an Agile team will reflect on the change, consider its repercussions on the project, and adjust their tasks and plans accordingly. This team sees a change request as an opportunity to support the organization's need for something different, rather than as a problem or setback. With this mindset, the team takes a positive attitude toward change.

The reflective approach is part of the Agile project management approach even when there are no changes to consider. The Agile team periodically reflects on projects and processes as a whole. By taking time to evaluate what is and isn't working and adjust appropriately, the Agile team is a learning team positioned to welcome change when it comes.

Embracing change is an element of the Agile approach's continuous attention to technical excellence and good design. Careful, considered design, including reflection on problems, changes, and processes makes it easier for the Agile team to accommodate change; the process anticipates changes and builds in the mechanism for evolving and adapting. When the team continuously monitors the project's technical components, major overhauls are often not needed because issues are caught and resolved while they are still small.

Technical excellence and good design might seem at odds with delivering working products frequently, but, in fact, they are interdependent. Rather than delivering a single completed product at the end of development, the Agile team delivers frequent iterations. This creates multiple opportunities for testing and feedback from project stakeholders, which leads to incremental improvements. The frequent feedback informs the design of the project and its technical requirements. The embrace of change and the intentional, iterative design feed into a cycle that reinforces the principles of Agile project management.

One side effect of welcoming change into your culture is that suddenly you start to see opportunities to further refine and streamline organizational processes, including reducing waste.

# A Culture of Trust

In addition to communicating openly, embracing change, and reducing waste, there's one final piece to the culture puzzle. Agile teams thrive on trust—not only among team members and managers but also in the project sponsors. Creating this culture of trust can be one of the hardest adjustments for organizations adopting Agile project management. It is at odds with a typical desire to control the process or relationship.

Making this shift results in more efficient, responsive production. Unfortunately, there's no handy trick—not even holding meetings while standing up or using color-coded project planning boards—to make it easier to build this trust. The shift must start at the top of the organization and percolate down. It also must be authentic. Appearing to share control without actually doing so undermines trust. People working in a culture of mistrust expend time and energy protecting themselves, sapping the energy that should be invested in accommodating change and responding quickly to project developments.

Trust within the organization is only part of the picture; trust in the project sponsor is also essential. When the sponsor is engaged across organizational and functional boundaries, an Agile team is set up for success. An engaged sponsor can make the hard decisions around prioritizing work and has the authority and courage to modify the project scope when new information is uncovered or when essential work is delayed.

Getting project sponsors involved with the planning and estimating process is a good way to build trust. A software development project manager shared this story with me:

Many years ago, we asked a project sponsor to participate in the estimation process. Though initially uncomfortable participating in a process she did not fully understand, she joined in and talked through the numbers with the team. We came to a feature request for online documentation. The project sponsor had estimated eight hours, but the developers on the team had estimated 40. Something was clearly off!

This provoked a conversation about the feature. The developers were thinking of sophisticated context-sensitive help, while the project sponsor was envisioning a simpler FAQ. The significant discrepancy in the numbers sparked a crucial conversation. After that, the sponsor was a willing participant in the project. And an important level of trust had been established between this sponsor and the team.

## Getting to an Agile Culture

The thought of overhauling the organizational culture at the same time you're shifting to Agile project management can be daunting. The Agile process itself can help.

A keystone of the Agile approach is looking at a large, overwhelming project and breaking it down into smaller, more manageable pieces.

Rather than wondering how to get all of this done at once, identify one change to the organizational culture that would have a positive impact on an Agile adoption. Figure out how to implement that one change. Once that change has been in place for a while, seek feedback:

- How do managers and developers feel about the change?
- What would they do differently?
- Has this change improved their productivity?
- Has it boosted morale or motivation?

Agile teams are highly collaborative. That means that one person should not bear the entire burden of making change. Brainstorm with others on how to implement Agile processes bit by bit. Collaboration turns the shift to Agile project management into an evolution, rather than an abrupt revolution.

Collaboration is also a way to approach incremental change in the organizational culture. Involving others is a great way to get their buy-in as well as a way to share responsibility. Everyone becomes a stakeholder with a commitment to the success of the Agile initiative—rather than a resentful employee who feels that change has been imposed from above.

Even with the best of intentions and most thoughtful approach, you're likely to hit some bumps. At these times, take another deep breath and remind yourself of the Agile process. Gather your team, evaluate the problem, come up with solutions, and, above all, embrace the change.

# Acknowledgments

This book is a culmination of more than a decade of practice, learning, and sharing.

The Agile Manifesto opens with the line, "We are uncovering better ways of developing software by doing it and helping others do it." This could not be truer of my journey with LLAMA, beginning by "uncovering" the secrets that my friends and colleagues in software development were using (thank you, Rob Houck, Dianne Marsh, Helene Gidley, and Rich Sheridan). It continued through years of "doing it" on projects with our clients who, in the early days, were patient with our growing pains (including Gary O'Neil, who at first declined to use our new "frou-frou" way of managing projects but ultimately became the supportive catalyst for so many of our ways of working), and who in recent years have seen Agile as an advantage. It's gratifying to now hear clients say, "We chose you because we know we're going to change our minds a lot and we knew that'd be OK with you."

The "helping others do it" is truly gratifying. A decade into our journey, thousands of people have attended a session, participated in a workshop, or read a book or article about our way of managing projects. (Had I known back then that this crazy idea of ours would take off, I would have started counting to have a more accurate number to capture the movement.) "LLAMAlumni" come from many countries on at least four continents, and I love getting photos and stories from people as they implement this way of working.

I could not ask for a better team of collaborators than the Torrance-Learning team, both current and past, who gamely give this a try, who wrestle with the implications of it, and who work with me to deepen the practice with their challenges and successes. Jen Vetter, Meg Fairchild, Alison Hass, Leanne Gee, Matt Kliewer, Dave Kerschbaum, Sue Kaba, Shannon Young, most recently Steve Wallag-Muno, and many others, have each had their hand in shaping LLAMA since this first rough whiteboard outline in the summer of 2012 when we gave it a name. We have built a business together based on Agile principles of flexibility, communication, sustainability, and transparency. Your spirit of generous collaboration (one of TorranceLearning's core values) is truly humbling and I appreciate your willingness to join me on this crazy ride.

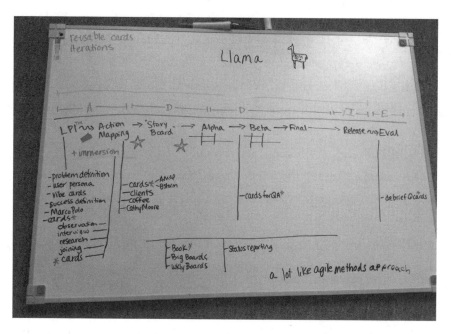

A special thanks to Jack Harlow and Hannah Sternberg for your careful editing and patience with my Agile approach to writing a book, and to Shirley Raybuck for the interior design. And a shout out to all the people who've encouraged me in the last few years to "write the damn book:" Marisa Smith, Catherine Juon, Cory Bouck, Michelle Massey Barnes, Kevin Daum, and Carla Torgerson . . . I finally sat down and did it!

Thank you to Zari Ozturk, Steve Wallag-Muno, and Matt Kliewer, whose graphical additions to the book have been essential in bringing the text to life.

Finally, I want to acknowledge the support from my family. Dad, your talent for writing about serious topics with a healthy dose of humanity and humor has been my inspiration throughout the writing of this book. Mom, thank you for your frequent trips to Michigan so I could be out on the road sharing LLAMA with others. And, Emily, yes, I'm doing the Skittles thing again. I love you.

# Appendixes

# The Agile Manifesto and 12 Principles for L&D Teams

## The Agile Manifesto

We are uncovering better ways of developing software by doing it and helping others do it. Through this work we have come to value:

- Individuals and interactions over processes and tools
- Working software over comprehensive documentation
- Customer collaboration over contract negotiation
- Responding to change over following a plan

That is, while there is value in the items on the right, we value the items on the left more.

## The 12 Principles

1. Our highest priority is to satisfy the customer through early and continuous delivery of valuable software.
2. Welcome changing requirements, even late in development. Agile processes harness change for the customer's competitive advantage.

3. Deliver working software frequently, from a couple of weeks to a couple of months, with a preference to the shorter timescale.

4. Businesspeople and developers must work together daily throughout the project.

5. Build projects around motivated individuals. Give them the environment and support they need, and trust them to get the job done.

6. Face-to-face conversation is the most efficient and effective method of conveying information to and within a development team.

7. Working software is the primary measure of progress.

8. Agile processes promote sustainable development. The sponsors, developers, and users should be able to maintain a constant pace indefinitely.

9. Continuous attention to technical excellence and good design enhances agility.

10. Simplicity—the art of maximizing the amount of work not done—is essential.

11. The best architectures, requirements, and designs emerge from self-organizing teams.

12. At regular intervals, the team reflects on how to become more effective, then tunes and adjusts its behavior accordingly.

# The 12 Principles for Learning Development Teams

As we did for the values from the Agile Manifesto, it can help to ground the Agile principles in their application to instructional design. Here's how each one can apply specifically to L&D teams.

**Our highest priority is to satisfy the customer through early and continuous delivery of valuable software.** This principle goes to the heart of iterative development. We don't take on a project, disappear into a black hole, and come back months later with a "final" product. We produce incremental "releases" of working products that the customer can try out. We're much more likely to get the end product right thanks to that input and feedback we've gotten throughout development. In the L&D context, we may release a large learning project in smaller phases rather than wait until an entire program is completed. Or, we may pilot a simple version of a learning experience in a fast-moving part of the organization to meet their needs quickly while learning from their results to apply to the rest of the organization.

**Welcome changing requirements, even late in development. Agile processes harness change for the customer's competitive advantage.** Software and L&D are both environments where changes should be assumed, expected, and accepted. By embracing this reality, Agile teams are able to meet changing needs, even if changes happen late in the development. The end result is therefore much more useful to the end users—the learners—and the organization.

**Deliver working [training] frequently, from a couple of weeks to a couple of months, with a preference to the shorter timescale. Working [training] is the primary measure of progress.** These two principles go hand-in-hand and I often discuss them together. Delivering early, frequent "working drafts" of the final product gives you an opportunity to get feedback; it's also a hedge against shifting priorities and budget cuts. If you've delivered something, even if it doesn't have all the bells and whistles on it you'd like, you've delivered value even when you couldn't "finish" a project. For this reason, Agile L&D teams will tend to deliver work in modules, focusing on the highest priority ones or those most ready to move forward faster.

**Business people and developers must work together daily throughout the project.** We once had a client who had an incredibly aggressive timeline and almost no budget for a project we really wanted to do. The project was to develop concussion awareness training for Michigan's youth sports coaches. At the time, I was coaching my daughter's ice hockey team; we had a roller derby player as a course developer; and one of our instructional designers coached community flag football. I had had a concussion a year prior myself playing hockey.

*We all really wanted to do this project.*

It was going to be a challenge, though, because the subject matter expert was a physician with a busy schedule. So we moved the client's project manager into our office. We gave her a desk, the Wi-Fi password, and all the coffee she could drink.

While perhaps extreme, this arrangement meant that whenever we had a question, she was right there to answer it. It also meant that she was in tune with our workflows and our work processes, so, as things changed, we adjusted together.

Moving a member of the client's team into your office might not be workable (or ideal), but some framework for frequent communication and quick responses to questions is essential. The closer the communication and collaboration, the easier it will be for all involved—stakeholders and developers alike—to make needed changes.

**Build projects around motivated individuals. Give them the environment and support they need, and trust them to get the job done.** Many L&D professionals who attend my workshops find that this principle resonates. It seems as though they are not often given the opportunity to be creative in their work or to work in an environment where they are trusted to make decisions.

By working *with* the business rather than against the business, by accepting change instead of resisting or preventing change, and by delivering frequently and delivering on time and in budget, Agile teams create an environment in which trust can be built.

**The most efficient and effective method of conveying information to and within a development team is face-to-face conversation.** This one is a tough sell in today's distributed environment of global teams and home-office workers. While remote work is certainly possible and often efficient, face-to-face communication remains the richest communication channel we have. Where possible and where critical, it's often worth it to make the extra effort to be together as a team. We insist on kicking off our projects face-to-face whenever possible, and we have never once regretted it.

**Agile processes promote sustainable development. The sponsors, developers, and users should be able to maintain a constant pace indefinitely.** No development process is perfectly smooth; Agile teams still have occasional late nights or long weekends. But planning by iteration makes it easier to manage the peaks and valleys of the work and maintain a sustainable pace.

**Continuous attention to technical excellence and good design enhances agility.** Agile project management supports, but does not inform, instructional design strategies. Solid instructional design and excellent project management are mutually reinforcing constructs; your projects need both. Remember, ADDIE is not an instructional design strategy either; it is a project management approach. Adopting an Agile approach does not infringe on instructional design strategies any more than using ADDIE does.

**Simplicity—the art of maximizing the amount of work not done—is essential.** With Agile, the focus is on meeting the needs of the customer. In L&D, that customer is the learner, the end user of the training. That focus is already a simplifying factor.

In the training development world, we tend to over-decorate and over-work some things. (You know you do it!) What's more, implementing extras makes the product harder to change as underlying needs shift in the future. By over-decorating, we do more work now, and we create more work for ourselves in the future—perhaps with little to no benefit to the learners.

**The best architectures, requirements, and designs emerge from self-organizing teams.** Many years ago at a NATO e-learning summit, I met a retired German military officer who was doing some training consulting to NATO. He asked me if my team hated Agile as much as his team did. Hated Agile? We love it! Taken aback, I asked him to explain.

He described how he had created all of the tasks and required team members to put status stickers on each of them. He described setting all of the project's work estimates for the team, and he told me how he laid out all of their tasks for them each week. He then said that his team told him that he was micromanaging them.

That's not Agile project management.

The part that he missed in all of this is that, on an Agile team, members work together to manage the project. The person responsible for a task estimates the time needed, for example—not the boss. While there is often a project manager, the entire team is responsible for making sure that the work is planned.

**At regular intervals, the team reflects on how to become more effective, then tunes and adjusts its behavior accordingly.** Agile teams call these discussions "retrospectives." In these conversations, the team examines not the product itself, but rather the process they used to get there.

# APPENDIX B

# Job Aids

## Project Kickoff Session Agenda

| Timing | Topic | Led By |
|---|---|---|
| 15 minutes | Introductions and Approach<br>• Introductions<br>• Agenda for the Day<br>• How We Use Agile | Project Manager |
| 1 hour | Define the Business Problem and Business Goal<br>• What is the business goal? How is it measured?<br>• What are the learners' goals? How are they measured? | Project Manager |
| 15 minutes | Break | |
| 1 hour | Define the Learner<br>• Create Learner Personas<br>• Select the Primary Learner Persona | Project Manager or Instructional Designer |
| 15 minutes | Break | |
| 1 hour | Define the Scope<br>• Action Mapping<br>• (Optional: User Stories) | Project Manager or Instructional Designer |
| 1 hour | Lunch | |
| 1 hour | Define Key Instructional Parameters | Instructional Designer |
| 1 hour | Define Key Project Parameters | Project Manager |
| 15 minutes | Break | |
| 30 minutes | Overall Project Budget and Timeline | Project Manager |
| 30 minutes | Iterations and Review Responsibilities | Project Manager or Instructional Designer |
| 30 minutes | Wrap Up and Next Steps | Project Manager |

# Learner Persona Questions List

Here are some sample questions to use as idea starters when creating a learner persona. Don't feel compelled to answer them all, as some will be more important to your project than others.

Demographics
- What is his/her name?
- What is his/her age?
- What is his/her gender?
- What is his/her primary language?
- What is his/her educational background?
- What is his/her marital and family status?
- Where does he/she live?

Professional Demographics
- What company does he/she work for?
- What is his/her job title?
- How long has he/she been with the organization?
- How long has he/she been in his/her current position?
- What is his/her income?
- How long has he/she been in the field of work?
- What job responsibilities does he/she have?
- Who does he/she interact with daily?
- How many people does he/she oversee?
- How much training and experience does he/she have with this topic?
- What end goals does he/she have related to the course?
- What experiences does he/she hope to have while taking the course?
- What career aspirations does he/she have?

- How does he/she feel about his/her current role with the organization?
- How often does he/she change jobs or employers?

## Connection to the Learning and Learning Approaches
- What motivated he/she to take the course?
- How often will he/she apply what he/she learned in the course?
- Has he/she taken training courses before?
- What type of computer does he/she typically use?
- What is his/her comfort level with computers/technology?
- What is his/her comfort level with the topic of this course?
- What other skills and abilities does he/she have?
- Does he/she have any disabilities or health problems?
- How open to change is he/she?
- Where will he/she take the course?
- What other types of professional development does he/she do?

## Away From Work
- How does he/she use social media?
- What does he/she like to do during spare time?
- What was the last book he/she read?
- What car does he/she drive?
- What is his/her favorite music?
- Where does he/she eat lunch?
- Is he/she more introverted or extroverted?
- How often does he/she exercise?

## Learner Persona Template

# LEARNER/USER PERSONA

| Name | Image |
|---|---|
| Demographics | |
| | Technology skills & preferences |
| Job & roles | |
| | Favorite brands, trends, culture |
| Motivations & comfort zones | |
| | Experience with this concept |
| Motto | |

# Written Status Report Outline

**STATUS REPORT:** Project Name

## Overview
(paragraph outlining the week's status in a nutshell)

## Activities We Completed Last Week
- Task 1

## Activities Planned for This Week
- Task 1

## Issues to Resolve/Open Questions
- **Green:** does not hinder our progress in the coming week.
- **Orange:** could hinder our progress in the coming week.
- **Red:** we are on full stop and cannot progress without resolution of the issue.

Issue 1 Description

## Estimate-to-Actuals
(graph and paragraph discussion)

# Capturing Retrospective Feedback

**Proud Moments**

**Embarrassed Moments**

**Budget/Timeline**

**Start-Stop-Continue**

| START | STOP | CONTINUE |
|-------|------|----------|
|       |      |          |
|       |      |          |
|       |      |          |
|       |      |          |

**To-Do Items**

# References

Beck, K., M. Beedle, A. van Bennekum, A. Cockburn, W. Cunningham, M. Fowler, J. Grenning, J. Highsmith, A. Hunt, R. Jeffries, J. Kern, B. Marick, R. Martin, S. Mellor, K. Schwaber, J. Sutherland, and D. Thomas. 2001. "Manifesto for Agile Software Development." http://agilemanifesto.org.

Chapman, B. 2010. *How Long Does It Take to Create Learning?* Chapman Alliance LLC.

Cohn, M. (N.d.) "About Mountain Goat Software" www.mountaingoat-software.com.

Defelice, R., and K. Kapp. 2018. "How Long Does It Take to Develop One Hour of Training? Updated for 2017." TD.org, January 9. www.td.org /insights/how-long-does-it-take-to-develop-one-hour-of-training -updated-for-2017.

Moore, C. 2017. *Map It! The Hands-On Guide to Strategic Training Design.* Montesa Press.

Reinerstein, D., and S. Thomke. 2012. "Six Myths of Product Development." *Harvard Business Review,* May. https://hbr.org/2012/05 /six-myths-of-product-development.

Rifkin, G. 1992. "Andersen Consulting's Culture of 'Clones.'" *New York Times,* September 6. www.nytimes.com/1992/09/06/business/andersen -consulting-s-culture-of-clones.html.

Rigby, D., J. Sutherland, and H. Takeuchi. 2016. "The Secret History of Agile Innovation." *Harvard Business Review,* April 20. https://hbr .org/2016/04/the-secret-history-of-agile-innovation.

Russell, L. 2016. *Project Management for Trainers,* 2nd Ed. Alexandria, VA: ATD Press.

Torrance, M. 2014. "Agile and LLAMA for ISD Project Management." TD at Work, November. www.td.org/td-at-work/agile-and-llama-for -isd-project-management.

# About the Author

Megan Torrance is CEO and founder of Torrance-Learning, which helps organizations connect learning strategy to design, development, data, and ultimately performance. Megan has more than 25 years of experience in learning design, deployment, and consulting. Megan and the TorranceLearning team are passionate about sharing what works in learning, so they devote considerable time to teaching and sharing techniques for Agile project management for instructional design and the Experience API. TorranceLearning hosts the xAPI Learning Cohort, a free, virtual 12-week learning-by-doing opportunity where teams form on the fly and create proof-of-concept xAPI projects.

Megan is the author of *The Quick Guide to LLAMA* and two *TD at Work* publications: "Agile and LLAMA for ISD Project Management" and "Making Sense of xAPI." She is a frequent speaker at conferences nationwide. TorranceLearning projects have won several Brandon Hall Group awards, the 2014 xAPI Hyperdrive contest at DevLearn, and back-to-back eLearning Guild DemoFest Best-In-Show awards in 2016 and 2017 with xAPI projects. TorranceLearning is a 2018 Michigan 50 Companies to Watch.

A graduate of Cornell University with a degree in communication and an MBA, Megan lives and works near Ann Arbor, Michigan.

# Index